Jim

INFO@JASCD.COM

Was William Wallace a Jacobite?

A Private Tour through Scotland's History

James A. Johnstone

First published by Private Tour Scotland in 2021
www.privatetourscotland.com

Publishing services provided by Lumphanan Press
www.lumphananpress.co.uk

Cover: The William Wallace monument, Stirling by Stefano Bobini (Shutterstock)

ISBN: 978-1-9196068-0-4

Printed by Imprint Digital, UK

Contents

Acknowledgements

I am extremely grateful to friends and family who have encouraged me in this endeavour but above all I want to thank my wife Rose, whose love and unfailing support is something I treasure – though even she may be relieved that, for a time at least, I will no longer be pestering her with "let me read this passage out to see what you think".

Our friend Deirdre Devlin, who is a television executive producer and author, was the first to read through an early draft of the complete manuscript and I am truly grateful for her overwhelmingly positive response and encouragement – not to mention the helpful suggestions she put forward in relation to areas where I refer to her native Ireland.

Within these pages I mention a private conversation I had a number of years ago with the eminent historian and author Professor James Hunter so I felt obliged to seek his permission before committing it to print. Given that he has written extensively on the subject of the Highland Clearances you can imagine my trepidation when it came to presenting him with my comparatively amateur work. However, my concerns caused me to overlook the fact that Jim Hunter is a true

Highland Gentleman. Not only did he read my chapter on the Highland Clearances, he also agreed to look through all of my original manuscript, and in the process, provided me with a few very useful pointers. Though I do not flatter myself that he necessarily agreed with all opinion expressed in this book I was elated when he too came back with highly positive comments, both in relation to the writing style and general content. I know this is not something he would normally undertake and can only hope he realises the extent of my gratitude and how much his comments have meant to me.

Introduction

As we drove through magnificent landscapes and spectacular rock formations, I was surrounded by the very familiar sound of excited chatter mixed with gasps of sheer amazement, so I really had to fight the urge to slip into my normal role as a driver/guide. I couldn't though since I had no greater knowledge than my fellow travellers, as this journey was far away from my native Scotland. It was March 2020 and my wife and I, in the company of our long-standing travel companions Alan and Carol Budgen, were slowly driving through the truly dramatic and "other worldly" landscape of Monument Valley on the Arizona/Utah border in the United States of America. Our first trip together had been in the year 2000, so this incredible journey through Arizona, Utah, and Nevada was our "20th Anniversary Trip". The easy company of four people who have known each other for a long time makes any trip enjoyable and this one was definitely no exception. However, there was a dark cloud on the horizon.

The potential threat from Covid-19 was certainly being widely discussed even before we left home and I would have to admit I was slightly concerned that it might adversely affect our touring business even though, at that point, there had been no cancellations, and new bookings for the summer of 2020 were still coming in. Being an election year in the USA, it was no surprise that most television news channels there were focusing on politics in a way that I have to admit we found a touch bewildering, but equally fascinating. Although Covid was being talked about, there was no sense of alarm, so we simply concentrated on enjoying our trip.

During the second week of our journey, the tone of reports started to change, and it became increasingly obvious that this virus was a serious threat on a worldwide basis. Two days before we were due to fly home, I got a call from my old friend Preston Epstein, who is one of the most respected people in the American travel industry. I was glad to hear from him, as nobody was better placed to give an indication of how things were looking in relation to international travel. His son Jonathan was also on the line and I immediately sensed an air of panic in his voice, but it was the calmer tones of Preston that really told me how serious the situation was, because for the first time in the twenty-five years I have known him, I was not hearing a shred of optimism. This is the man I would call for encouragement to counter my natural Scottish pessimism and it never failed to work – till now.

Jonathan had every reason to panic, and Preston had every reason to be pessimistic, as their office staff were now being flooded with cancellations. On the Saturday of our departure from McCarran International Airport in Nevada, we took a drive through the crazy busy Las Vegas Strip – days later, it was a ghost town. As the United Kingdom, and much of the world, went into lockdown, the flood of travel cancellations turned into a tsunami. Like so many other businesses, we simply ground to a halt and, as we now know, it will take a long time for the tourism and travel industry to get back to where we were in 2019. However, the industry will come back and I, for one, look forward to the day when I can be out on the road touring round Scotland with guests, though tragically that will be of little consequence to the many families who lost loved ones to this truly horrible virus.

It is hard to find positives in the general misery of 2020, but it could be that some of us found we had time on our hands; time to do something other than the work which, till now, has dominated our lives. This book is one such example since it started out as notes to give to guests at the end of a touring trip, but with the gift of time, I got slightly carried away.

1

Making of a Driver/Guide

"How did you come to be in this line of work?" When you bear in mind that I am driving and guiding people on a touring trip throughout Scotland, you might think the number one question would relate to history, culture, religion, or even politics, but no, the number one question is frequently about me – their driver/guide. I mostly travel with couples or small groups, up to a maximum of six, and they tend to be family or friends who already know each other well. However, they now want to know more about the person they have just met, the person who will be part of their lives throughout the days they will spend touring, so it is not long before the subtle, and not so subtle, enquiries begin. To be fair, it is perfectly understandable, so at an early stage in any trip, I am ready with a "brief" personal history.

After leaving school at the age of eighteen, my first few years in gainful employment were mostly spent as a travelling salesman, first in the food industry then later in motor vehicle parts, where I ended up with a sales territory that covered a large part of Scotland. The travelling part was great, but I was beginning to struggle with the selling side of the job and had to face up to the fact that I was not actually very good at it, so that particular career kind of gave me up. At twenty-four years old, I had no job, no prospects, and no money. Following an increasingly uncomfortable and poverty-stricken period of unemployment, I decided to take the first job available and that turned out to be a delivery driver for a bakery and restaurant chain. I did this for about a year and now look back on that period with very fond memories, for the simple reason that it is the people you work with that often help make a job enjoyable. Being honest with myself, I should probably admit it was also the year when I started to grow up, as saving money finally became more important than spending it. A young lady by the name of Rosemary MacQueen managed one of the bakeries' restaurants and I tended to have more of my coffee breaks there than anywhere else. Yes, you have guessed correctly, she later became Mrs Rosemary Johnstone, and still is, I am glad to say.

Though well aware that I had to tidy up my career path, I had no idea where it was leading, so now chose to apply for a taxi operator's licence in my hometown of Inverness and subsequently entered into the world of self-employment, though to be honest, at the time, I was still looking upon this as a stop-gap measure.

In the summer of 1982, I took a little time out and went on a trip to America with a small group of friends. With six of us crammed into a Chevrolet Station Wagon, we travelled from Miami to New Orleans, Memphis, and Nashville, among other places, before ending our journey back in Florida at Fort Lauderdale. It was a fantastic trip that we all enjoyed, but it was also an experience that would ultimately change my career. Having newly started working as a taxi driver in Inverness, I could not help noticing the number of taxis in Nashville offering private "taxi tours" taking in the homes of country music stars. In the Highlands of Scotland, we have great attractions including Loch Ness, Culloden Battlefield, and Cawdor Castle, so why were we not doing something like this?

Though self-employed, I was a member of a cooperative group that ran our taxi booking office and this was managed by an elected committee, so I carefully prepared a written submission on the subject of fixed price taxi tours as soon as I got back and waited anxiously to hear the outcome. Unfortunately, the company's elderly decision makers dismissed the whole idea when they came to the line where I introduced the word "cost". Now I know that sounds slightly ageist, and yes, when I was in my mid-twenties I almost certainly was, but I am now kind of elderly myself and I still think they were a bunch of old fuddy-duddies. I was annoyed but determined, so at the following Annual General Meeting, I put myself up for election and, to my amazement, gained a place on the management team. Now, the most effective committee would probably consist of three members with two permanently absent, but that is not easy to arrange, so I had to fight my corner in the traditional way and eventually persuaded them to give me a budget to spend on promotional leaflets. I think my fellow committee members felt this was the equivalent of giving the wee boy a lollipop in the hope that they could get some peace, but I didn't care, as I had won. For the moment, I am going to set aside my shy, retiring, modest Highland characteristics to declare that it was a massive success and, for a time at least, my fellow taxi drivers thought I was the greatest thing since sliced bread. Much as I enjoyed the praise (who doesn't?), I was very aware I had created something that would benefit many but would not really bring much in the way of personal reward. Unfortunately, I lacked the resources to do it alone.

I chose to resolve this by going into a partnership with a friend who showed an interest, though he was keen to provide more of a touring package aimed at larger group sizes. Sufficient to say it ultimately did not work out, as a partnership like this means permanently compromising and I have to admit I was probably the one least willing to do so. I am glad to say that our friendship survived even if the partnership did not.

I then went back to my original idea, but this time decided to take it more upscale by creating a Chauffeur Driven Car Service that was to specialise in private touring. Rose and I spent everything we had on luxury vehicles, so for the next few years, we had expensive cars in our driveway but struggled to find money to pay household bills. Despite those early difficulties, we slowly built up a network of contacts and the business started to grow. Along the way, we were incredibly fortunate to find great drivers and the all-important driver/guides who were to become a vital part of the service we provided. That is the short answer to the question, "How did you come to be in this line of work?" Now would you like to hear the long answer? Okay, perhaps not.

Being a driver/guide in Scotland truly is one of the best jobs in the world, and I say this as someone who has been doing that very job for almost forty years. During an average five – to six-day trip, we cover a large part of the country and enjoy great conversations about historical figures such as William Wallace,

Robert the Bruce, Stuart kings, John Knox, Mary de Guise, Mary Queen of Scots, and many, many others. Inevitably, at some point, we talk about the Scottish Reformation and the Scottish Enlightenment, so yes, that brings in religion and politics. We have to talk about these latter subjects, as they played a vital role in shaping the Scotland I live in today. Add in visits to places of interest, cultural exploration, not to mention truly spectacular scenery, and you begin to understand why my "job" is so much better than working for a living! Though I live in the Scottish Highlands, I have, over the years, started and ended trips in various locations throughout the British Isles. Scotland is, of course, my main "stomping ground" and Edinburgh is probably the most frequent starting point for a trip.

Most of the guests I meet up with in Edinburgh are borderline exhausted, as they have normally spent the previous day or two walking in the city. They will almost certainly have done the "Royal Mile Rumba" where you zig-zag on the mile between Edinburgh Castle and Holyrood Palace, trying to avoid collision with a mass of visitors all trying to do the same thing. Much as people (myself included) love the City of Edinburgh, it can actually be quite a relief to get away from it – particularly during midsummer. We get to know each other as we wind our way out of the city and I quickly gain a feel for what may, or may not, interest the guests I will be spending time with during the days ahead. It is not long before great conversations begin on a wide range of subjects depending on interests, the areas we are travelling through, and locations where we might stop and visit.

Though we generally have a basic itinerary, the type of private touring I am fortunate to be involved in allows for a tremendous degree of flexibility. Now that really is great for the purposes of touring, but if I were to try and write this book in the same way, it would become even more of a jumbled-up mess than it is probably going to be anyway. I am, therefore, going to stick with history as the primary narrative though I have to admit my butterfly mind will take us down the occasional side road.

For the avoidance of doubt, I have to point out that I am not a historian. However, I am endlessly fascinated by Scottish history and will forever be grateful to the real historians and historical writers who have given all of us the benefit of their meticulous research into so many aspects of past life in Scotland. Authors such as James Hunter, Niall Ferguson, Tom Devine, Michael Lynch, Michael Fry, Fitzroy Maclean, Antonia Fraser, John Prebble, and Arthur Herman are among those who have helped give me the essential knowledge I need to guide visitors through this wonderful little country.

History is, of course, subjective, so there are times when we have to apply our own interpretation and I would have to say that I am now old enough, and ugly enough, to give an opinion when required. I am inclined to say the same with religion and politics though we are sadly at a point, certainly in the United Kingdom and United States of America, where people are so bitterly divided, we all have to tread a little more carefully. It is not a comfortable situation, so we can only hope that it will prove to be a very brief period in our history. Being a driver/guide in Scotland, I cannot really avoid talking about present-day Scottish politics, as our guests, understandably, want to know more about the history of the independence movement, where we are with it now, and where we are likely heading. There are times when it is just too painful to stay sitting on the fence.

2

The Tour Begins

In common with many other countries, you will find that people in Scotland spend a lot of time talking about the weather and generally commiserating with each other on how bad it is or is going to be. Unfortunately, we do not really do optimism in Scotland, particularly in the Highlands, so we tend to dwell on the wet, miserable summer weather we sometimes experience rather than the many glorious sunny days that we do actually enjoy every year. On one of these warm summer mornings, several years ago, I was sitting in a coffee shop in Edinburgh enjoying a bit of "me time" before heading to the Howard Hotel on Great King Street to meet up with my guests for the beginning of a seven-day tour. I used the time to do a final check through of the details of the trip and also to commit the guest names to memory. Regrettably, I no longer hold that information and have to admit that I cannot remember their names. Although, as with many of my guests over the years, I have a perfectly clear recollection of how they looked and sounded.

We introduced ourselves in the hotel foyer, loaded their luggage in the car, and slowly wound our way through the Edinburgh morning traffic. As I write this, the names Bill and

Helen come to mind, so I am going to go with that – who knows, it might even be right. Bill was in his early seventies and still a practicing lawyer in Michigan (there are an awful lot of lawyers in America), and his similarly aged wife Helen was a retired teacher. In common with so many of our guests, they were great company from the outset and clearly ready to enjoy the days we would spend together. Both had an obvious interest in Scottish history, as the questions were coming thick and fast within the first few miles of our journey. We had just crossed the Firth of Forth when Bill asked: "Jim, this may be a dumb question, but was William Wallace a Jacobite?" Now, to most people, that would indeed be in the dumb question category, as there was a gap of almost 400 years between the death of William Wallace and the birth of the Jacobite cause, so the direct answer was a very definite no. However, I sensed that he already knew the factual answer and the more we talked the more I realised that was indeed the case. From what he had already learned, it appeared to him that much of early Scottish history was on a constantly repeating loop where only the leading figures changed during periods of near identical struggles. He had thrown in that seemingly ridiculous question in the hope that, as their driver/guide, I might help them pull together the threads of their existing knowledge. Over the course of the next six days, we visited a number of interesting locations, enjoyed spectacular scenery, and spent many journeys dipping in and out of conversations covering the 400-year period I just mentioned – plus a great deal more. It was one among many memorable trips filled with great conversations though Bill's question is one I have never forgotten. I knew exactly where he was coming from even if I did not entirely agree with his analysis, and it did provide an interesting baseline for a tour through Scottish history.

Travelling along the Fife coast, as I did that day with Bill and Helen, you come to the small town of Kinghorn, which apparently means "Head of the marsh" (one for the useless information file). Just before reaching the town, you come across a sizeable monument. It is barely a step back from the roadside, and immediately behind runs a railway track. All told, this monument to King Alexander III of Scotland carries an air of neglect though perhaps you should not be surprised, as most people, including many Scots, have no idea who he was. Personally, I find this to be rather sad, as his life, and death, relates directly to the beginning of a story leading to names and events from Scottish history that came to be known worldwide.

3

The Tragedy of Alexander III

Alexander III succeeded his father in 1249 when he was only seven years old. By the time he reached the grand age of ten, he was married to the eleven-year-old daughter of Henry III of England. As you might guess, this was arranged between the English king and the "Guardians of Scotland", or regents, who were appointed to rule on Alexander's behalf during his minority. These men were senior nobles who frequently governed in their own interests rather than that of the young king, so when he came of age, he had to be strong, really strong, to firmly establish his authority. He was, and he did. Even at ten years old, he had the courage to stand up to his father-in-law, Henry, and refused to pay homage to him as his feudal superior. As an adult, in his mid-twenties, he successfully repelled a Norwegian attack in 1263, and subsequently arranged a treaty that brought the Western Isles (Hebridean Islands) and the Isle of Man under his control. Since he was also at peace with England, not least through his marriage ties, this was close to a "Golden Period" in Scotland.

The marriage to Henry of England's daughter produced three children, two boys (Alexander and David) and a girl

(Margaret), so he had an heir and a spare as well as a "useful" daughter. Yes, that is a pretty horrible description, but it was, unfortunately, a fact of life for most young princesses. They were often little more than a bargaining tool to further the diplomatic and dynastic interests of their father. In 1281, at the age of twenty, Margaret was married to the adolescent, spotty-faced thirteen-year-old King Erik of Norway. She must have been thrilled. She had no choice, however, and two years later gave birth to a daughter. Sadly, Margaret died, probably from complications following the birth, but she had given Alexander a grandchild (also Margaret). Fate now began to take an unfortunate turn for Alexander. By the time young Margaret was three years old, Alexander III of Scotland had been pre-deceased by his wife and all three of his children. His only heir was now the infant grandchild in Norway who would from then on be known as "the Maid of Norway".

Alexander was barely in his mid-forties, so there was every reason to be confident that he would yet produce more children and ideally, of course, a male heir. In October 1285, he married twenty-two-year-old Yolande of Dreux. This apparently beautiful young French lady, who came from an impeccable noble line, appeared to be a good choice and the marriage returned confidence that all would be okay. The King and his new bride settled in Kinghorn Castle during the early months of their marriage and, perhaps not surprisingly, Alexander was reluctant to be apart from her any longer than was absolutely necessary. However, he did still have matters of state to attend to, so in March 1286, he travelled to Edinburgh to meet with his advisors. By March 19th, business matters were concluded, and he was anxious to get back to Kinghorn to celebrate his wife's birthday the following day.

It was a wild, windy day and as the threatening storm grew stronger, the boatman at the ferry crossing on the Firth of Forth tried to persuade the King to wait until the weather improved. There were, of course, no bridges crossing the Firth at that time, so the only alternative to the ferry would have been the bridge crossing the River Forth at Stirling. Given that this would add around forty miles to their journey, the King was not taking no for an answer, so they set sail across the Firth. The crossing must have been pretty scary, but they somehow landed safely on the other side. Alexander and his small entourage then rode their horses at full gallop along the coast of Fife towards Kinghorn. At some point, Alexander became separated from the main group, but he was in a hurry, so decided to ride on alone. When the others reached Kinghorn Castle, they were surprised to find their Lord and Master was not ahead of them. As the night wore on, this surprise turned to concern – something was wrong. When daylight appeared, the lifeless body of King Alexander III of Scotland was found on the shore, almost within sight of his castle – his horse had stumbled on a cliff path and he plunged to his death. Alexander had been a popular king, so there was a genuine sense of shock. However, as that shock subsided, it gave way to a realisation that there was now a potential crisis in the line of succession. His widow was pregnant, so there was still a chance that she might give birth to a male heir, but sadly this was not to be, as Queen Yolande lost her child. The only surviving heir to the throne of Scotland was now Alexander's infant granddaughter, the Maid of Norway.

When, during the early 1960s, British prime minister Harold Macmillan was asked what could possibly undermine his government, he famously gave the very simple, not to mention very British, reply, "Events, dear boy, events." The path of history is, of course, a series of events and we can be certain that the untimely death of Alexander III was one that completely changed the course of Scottish history. Again, I cannot help wondering why the best we can do today, by way of remembering this king and subsequently this event, is a modest, neglected, badly located monument.

4

Edward I of England (Longshanks)

Although the young Margaret would initially remain in Norway, she was the rightful, albeit uncrowned, Queen of Scotland. Until she could be brought to Scotland for her coronation, nobles appointed as the Guardians of Scotland would rule on her behalf. Once again, the country would be governed by men who were all too ready to mix their loyalty to the Scottish Crown with a hefty dollop of self-interest. Through hereditary rights and dynastic marriage, many Scottish nobles also held estates in England, so ultimate loyalty could be complicated. Edward I of England, also known as "Longshanks" (he was a tall man with long legs), was well aware of these complications and clearly sensed an opportunity. He believed himself to be the feudal superior of Scotland, as did previous English kings, but he was going to press this more firmly than any monarch had done before.

Edward proposed a marriage between his young son (also Edward) and Margaret, the Maid of Norway. Inter-marriage between Scottish and English royalty was nothing unusual, but this would be different, as the male heir to the English throne would be married to the female heir to the Scottish throne. Given that a king ranked higher than a queen, it would ultimately mean a union of the Crowns under King Edward II when, in due course, he succeeded his father. Without question, this was a dilemma for Scottish nobles, but eventually, in 1290, they signed a treaty with Edward Longshanks that paved the way for this marriage between his six-year-old son and the now seven-year-old Maid of Norway. Though a significant part of the negotiations took place directly between King Edward I of England and King Erik II of Norway, Scottish nobles had it written into the treaty that, when the time came, Scotland and England would, yes, be under one king but would also remain as two separate, self-governing countries. Edward agreed but almost certainly had never intended to honour that particular part of the treaty.

As a driver/guide, I am well used to hearing the phrase "I have a question", as many of our American guests have a tendency to use this prefix before asking the actual question. Believe me, the more I hear this, the happier I am, as it generally means they are interested and engaged. When I am telling this particular story, the most frequent question is "Were young Edward and Margaret close cousins?" The answer is, of course, yes, and it has to be said that it was not terribly unusual though Edward had sought and was granted papal dispensation for this marriage. This frequently sparks off a conversation regarding the potential consequences of royal marriages between close family members throughout history though I, as a loyal British subject, could not possibly comment.

With everything now in place, Edward sent a ship to take Margaret, the Maid of Norway, to Scotland, where she would be formally crowned before her marriage to his son. She was taken ill en route and when they stopped off at St Margaret's Hope in Orkney, her condition rapidly deteriorated. Sadly, young Margaret passed away. Rather than continue, the ship returned to Norway for her distraught father to identify his daughter's body. This was a very real human tragedy, especially for King Erik who was himself little more than a teenager, but it was a tragedy of a different kind for Scotland, as it left the country with no obvious heir to the throne.

Even before the death of Margaret, the Maid of Norway, there were a few Scottish nobles who felt they had the hereditary right to be the next King of Scotland, but after her death they really started to come out of the woodwork. No fewer than thirteen serious contenders now came forward to press their claim. As various factions gathered, it was clear that Scotland was on the brink of civil war. To some extent, Scottish nobles probably felt rudderless, so we should perhaps not be too ready to criticise when we learn that they now chose to turn to the "superior" figure of a monarch to advise them. That person was, of course, Edward I of England. By invitation, he came in to adjudicate on who among the many claimants should be chosen as the Scottish king. Like some medieval version of "Scotland's got Talent", the contestants were first whittled down to four, then to two. The final two were senior Scottish nobles John Balliol and Robert Bruce. In the Great Hall of Berwick Castle in 1292, Edward gave his approval to John Balliol. Three days later, Balliol was crowned at Scone Abbey, near Perth. It was the 30th of November – St Andrew's Day (Scotland's patron saint). It is often suggested that Edward Longshanks felt Balliol would be easier to manipulate than Bruce and that may well have been the case, but the truth is that Balliol did have a slightly better claim. He was the great-great-great-grandson of the revered 9th Century king, David I of Scotland.

Many years ago, there was one "I have a question" that threw me slightly. It was quite simply: "Did this John Balliol have anything to do with the famous Balliol College at Oxford University?" I had to look it up and was amazed to find that there was indeed a connection. King John Balliol's father (also John Balliol) was a major landowner in the north of England who, at some point, fell out with the Bishop of Durham. Apparently, by way of penance, he was persuaded to fund a building at Oxford for a new college that today bears his name.

Between Edward Longshanks pulling the strings and openly hostile Scottish nobles, who still believed Balliol to be the wrong choice, he never really stood a chance. Even a strong, powerful figure would have struggled to establish his authority and, by all accounts, Balliol was never going to fit that description. His rule as king was always going to be overshadowed by the dominating Edward. Throughout 1294, England was preparing for war with France, so Edward let it be known that his nobles were required to finance an army and provide the men to fight. As far as Edward was concerned, King John Balliol of Scotland was little more than one of his nobles, so he fully expected that a Scottish army would be raised to fight for England. This was a step too far for Scottish nobility. In October 1295, a dozen senior Scottish nobles signed a treaty with France that was basically a statement of mutual protection. If England invaded France, Scotland would invade England. The "Auld Alliance", as it came to be known, was pretty much based on the principle that "your enemy is my enemy". Not surprisingly, Edward was furious and laid the blame firmly at the door of Balliol. As he saw it, this ungrateful Scottish king, who Edward himself had actually appointed, was not capable of controlling his own rebellious nobles. It was only a matter of time before the fearsome wrath of Edward Longshanks would descend upon the people of Scotland. The Scots prepared for war.

Having learned about the history of Scotland from novels, television, and cinema, many of our guests are under the impression that there has been perpetual conflict between Scotland and England down through the ages. In truth, there have been long periods of peace, and prior to 1296, Scotland was generally accepted as a separate independent country with its own recognised monarchs. Yes, there was hostility and land raids between Scotland and England, resulting in English monarchs declaring their feudal superiority, but there had never really been any serious attempt to consolidate the various parts that made up the British Isles. Even the Romans gave up on that idea. However, this all changed under the rule of Edward I of England. Whatever we may say about him, we cannot deny that he had a vision, though unlike visionary politicians of today, he did not need to waste any time on whether or not he could bring the people with him. He had already subjugated Wales and was now determined to do the same to Scotland. Relations between Scotland and England definitely took a serious turn for the worse during the reign of Edward I and arguably things were never to be quite the same again.

In March 1296, Edward Longshanks sent an army north to the Scottish border town of Berwick-on-Tweed, where only a few years before he had announced John Balliol as the new King of Scotland. His army camped nearby and gave notice to the townspeople that they must surrender within three days. When they refused, Edward's army descended upon the town in an orgy of sickening violence. Some records suggest that as many as 15,000 men, women, and children were killed in the carnage that followed. Even if the true figures were less, as they almost certainly were, this was still nothing short of a brutal massacre. The "shock and awe" tactics adopted by Edward were, of course, a very deliberate choice, as they carried a clear message: this is what happens when you attempt to defy Edward I of England. He then ordered that the town be rebuilt and repopulated with subjects from England.

Although today Berwick-on-Tweed is a beautiful coastal town in the far north of England, it was in the frontline of many struggles between England and Scotland from the 10th to the 15th Century. This small town changed hands on no fewer than thirteen occasions during that period. It was taken for the final time in 1482 by England's King Edward IV and has remained an English town ever since. Fourteen years later, a Treaty of Perpetual Peace, that gave specific mention of Berwick, was signed between England and Scotland. It stated that Berwick-on-Tweed was "of the Kingdom of England but not in it", so, thereafter, the town had to be separately named in any royal proclamation. As a result, Berwick was duly described in this way upon the declaration of war with Russia, signed by Queen Victoria in 1853. However, it was not mentioned in the peace treaty signed in 1856, so, technically, Berwick remained at war with Russia. This situation was not resolved until a summit was held in 1966 between a Russian diplomat and the then Mayor of Berwick. I am sure it was a massive relief for the people of Russia when they were told that Berwick-on-Tweed was no longer likely to invade Russian soil.

Whenever I am touring anywhere close to Berwick-on-Tweed, I always try to make time for a visit, not least for its rich history. As the name suggests, it sits on the River Tweed, which is crossed by a number of impressive bridges including the Royal Border Rail Bridge, dating from 1850. Though walled towns are not unusual throughout the United Kingdom, there are few with walls as intact as those that surround Berwick-on-Tweed.

Within weeks of Edward I taking Berwick, he had his army march some thirty miles up the coast to take Dunbar Castle. Under King John Balliol, Scotland was advancing its preparation for the inevitable war with England and by now had gathered a significant army. Forces sent by Balliol to prevent the capture of Dunbar Castle confronted Edward's superior forces and suffered a resounding defeat. It would appear that nothing could stop Edward Longshanks as his army swept through Scotland, taking control of all its major castles. Balliol had no choice but to surrender and throw himself upon Edward's mercy. The other soubriquet applied to Edward I was "Hammer of the Scots" and, given the way he acted, it is very easy to see why. Balliol was stripped of his crown, royal regalia, and royal garments, hence the name given to him of "Toom Tabard", or empty pockets, as he was left with nothing. He was then taken as a prisoner to the Tower of London. The Scottish Crown

Jewels and any documents relating to Scotland's monarchy were taken to England, but even more symbolically, the Stone of Scone was taken from Scone Abbey in Perth and placed under the Throne of England in Westminster Abbey. It may well be little more than a lump of rock, but it was a very important lump of rock upon which all Scottish kings were seated during their coronation.

Edward Longshanks was not finished yet, as he now demanded that all land-owning Scottish nobles sign an oath of allegiance to him. This came to be known as the "Ragman's Roll", and guess what, it was dutifully signed by virtually every relevant Scottish noble. Again, we really should put this in the context of the time in order to understand why so many in Scotland were willing to sign this document. To a great extent, it was down to the land many Scottish nobles held in England, so, of course, there was an element of divided loyalties. They stood to lose their lands and their position, not to mention the danger to their families – and themselves. Yes, there would have been elements of naked greed, but it is too simplistic to say that was the only motive. Edward appears to have concluded that his mission was now accomplished and chose to withdraw, leaving appointed English officials, assisted by a few "loyal" Scottish nobles, to rule Scotland. Of one thing he was certain – there would be no more Scottish kings. Edward I of England was now in charge of Scotland's destiny.

5

The Stone of Scone

Stone of Scone, Stone of Destiny, Jacobs Pillow, the Tanist Stone, the Coronation Stone. Whatever you want to call it (I will settle for the Stone of Scone), this piece of rock has almost become part of the DNA of the Scottish people. In many ways, this is down to Edward I of England, as he stole a little of the soul of Scotland when he took away the stone that acted as a throne for all Scottish kings during their coronation. There was, and still is, a mythical element to the Stone of Scone, as its true origins are shrouded in the mists of time. Did it come to Scotland from the holy land via Egypt, Spain, and Ireland? Or did an early Scottish king just decide this particular lump of rock looked quite comfortable? Edward I of England knew full well what the stone meant to Scotland, so he had that "symbolic power" transferred to England and placed under the throne at Westminster. It was to stay there for a very long time.

Four independence-supporting Scottish students decided to enforce their message in the early hours of Christmas Day in 1950 by stealing the Stone of Scone from underneath the throne in Westminster Abbey. Even allowing for much lower levels of security existing at that time, it is quite amazing that they were able to drag this very heavy stone out of the abbey into a waiting car and drive off without being seen. Given the weight involved, it was a mighty task for three people (one waited outside with the car), so, not surprisingly, the stone was dropped at one point, causing it to split into two parts, but they were undeterred and carried on with their mission. The abbey raiders secretly hid the two parts of the stone somewhere in London and headed for home.

When the theft was discovered, King George VI (our current queen's father) was "greatly distressed", the government were in a blind panic, and the police were embarrassed. The border between England and Scotland was closed for the first time in 400 years so that all vehicles crossing could be searched. Freight transport operators were told to look out for any suspicious packages – well, very heavy ones at least. No doubt there were many people throughout the United Kingdom who shared the King's distress, but I think it might also be fair to say that many more were mildly amused even if they did not actually condone the students' actions. The "amusement" may have been slightly more prevalent in Scotland. When things started to calm down and the roadblocks were lifted, the students returned to collect the stone and took it to Glasgow, where a stonemason repaired the damage they had caused. The police were getting nowhere with their investigation and must have been mightily relieved when, four months after the stone was taken from Westminster, they got a lead suggesting that it was at Arbroath Abbey. The students chose to leave this very symbolic stone at a very symbolic location (more about that later). It was returned to Westminster Abbey and again placed under the throne. By now the police knew who the four students were, and each was interviewed. However, no charges were ever pressed, as the government of the day, perhaps wisely, did not want to give oxygen to the flames of Scottish nationalism. One of the four, Ian Hamilton, was a law student who went on to be a successful Glasgow lawyer and Queen's Counsel.

The stone was finally returned to Scotland in 1996 and, if we are going to be honest, that was little more than a brazen attempt to appease the independence movement which by then was very much on the rise in Scotland. As we now know, it did not work. There are plans for the stone to be displayed in a Perth museum, but for now, it takes pride of place in an exhibition at Edinburgh Castle though it has been agreed that it will briefly be returned to Westminster for any future coronations, e.g., Prince Charles or Prince William (in due course). However, there has always been a suspicion that the monks at Scone Abbey hid the real stone and quickly created a copy for Edward to "steal". Now that would mean the stone that was ceremonially returned to Scotland after 700 years is actually a copy. We all love a bit of mystery, but geologists have recently declared that this block of red sandstone was almost certainly quarried in Perthshire – close to where Scone Abbey would have stood in 1296. Bang goes another conspiracy theory. Or, then again, does it?

It is worth mentioning that the Stone of Destiny is still deemed to be relevant in some nationalist circles though it is hard to understand why, as many ardent supporters of independence for Scotland are also republicans, so would presumably have no use for it. Perhaps they still see it as a "symbol of Scottish power" whereas others may simply see it now as a "powerful symbol of Scotland".

6

Wars of Independence (William Wallace)

Edward I of England was confident that any minor resistance to his domination of Scotland could be easily dealt with and that was pretty much the case until a certain William Wallace appeared on the scene. What we think we know about Wallace mostly comes from a very, very long poem, 'The Wallace', written in the late 15th Century (around 150 years after his death) by an author called Blind Harry. It was, even then, heavily based on what we might today call urban myth. However, it was a popular mythology that continues to resonate, so we have to acknowledge that Blind Harry laid the foundation for how Wallace came to be portrayed. This creativity reached a new level in the 1995 film *Braveheart* which I have to admit was a great film but equally have to say it was very much a work of fiction. It is tempting to use the currently fashionable terms of "fake news" and "alternative facts", as they relate to entertainment rather that education. Though I mention this in order to create some context of reality, it should not detract from what we do know about William Wallace, as there is adequate evidence to suggest that he was indeed a great patriotic Scot who was ready and willing to fight for what he believed in.

Anyone who refused to sign the Ragman's Roll was to be declared an outlaw and an enemy of Edward I of England, so even today many highlight the fact that William Wallace's name does not appear. Again, we do not really know why it was not on the document, or even if this is of any real significance. In more recent times, it has been suggested that his father was Alan Wallace, a tenant of the Crown in Ayrshire. The name of Alan Wallace did appear on the Ragman's Roll, so would his sons (including William) have been classed as outlaws? If we go with traditional wisdom and accept that his father was Sir Malcolm Wallace of Elderslie, in Renfrewshire, it is true that this family name does not appear. However, as the third son, William did not inherit the title or any land, so at that time, he was plain William Wallace. Whatever his origins, we do know that Wallace was not born into the noble ruling classes. It has even been suggested that, as a very young man, he had strayed towards the "wrong side of the law" before venturing into the turbulent politics of the time. Either way, if he had not already been declared an outlaw, he soon would be. In May 1297, Wallace and a small group of followers killed Sir William Heselrig, the English Sheriff of Lanark. No one can be certain why this happened and there is absolutely no evidence to support the story that it was an act of revenge for the murder of his wife. In fact, we don't know if Wallace was even married, but we do know he was now a wanted man. He was however, very clearly, a leader of men who inspired confidence to the extent that he soon gained the support required for a full-scale rebellion.

Rebellion was also stirring in the north of Scotland under the leadership of Andrew de Moray, or simply Andrew Murray, as we will now refer to him. Murray came from a prominent, well-connected, land-owning family based in the Highlands of Scotland. He and his father, Sir Andrew de Moray, had fought against Edward's army at Dunbar, where both were taken prisoner. Though Sir Andrew was incarcerated in the Tower of London, his son was imprisoned at Chester, from where he somehow managed to escape and make his way home to the family seat of Avoch Castle (also known as Ormond Castle) on the Black Isle. If for any reason you have to pronounce that name, it comes out as a very Scottish-sounding "Och". I know, how on earth do you get that sound from Avoch? Young Andrew Murray was determined to continue the fight and promptly set about raising an army in the north. Like Wallace, it is clear that Murray could inspire others to follow him. Everything we know about him suggests he was not just a great warrior but also an astute tactician and a master of guerrilla warfare. Wallace was, of course, fighting a similar campaign in the south. We do not know for certain, but it is likely that there would have been some element of communication between Murray and Wallace before their forces finally combined prior to the Battle of Stirling Bridge. It would be wrong to suggest that they were the only ones showing resistance to English occupation, as other nobles such as Macduff of Fife and Robert Wishart (Bishop of Glasgow), alongside a young Robert Bruce and James Stewart, the High Steward, were also involved in active rebellion. However, it might also be fair to add that Wallace, unlike most senior Scottish nobles, was determined to fight till the English occupation was brought to an end; there would be no compromise, and no capitulation. Though Murray came from a more noble line than Wallace, it would appear that he was similarly minded.

By late 1297, Edward had had enough and sent an army north to deal with the troublesome Scots. These forces were led by the Earl of Surrey, Edward's governor in Scotland, as Edward himself was otherwise occupied fighting in France. Surrey had, at least, the passive support of some within the ranks of Scottish nobility and the active support of a few such as the Earl of Lennox and James Stewart, the High Steward (who by now had switched sides), so it is hardly surprising that he was confident of victory whether by negotiation or in battle. The English army was aiming to relieve Dundee Castle, which had for some time been under siege, and planned a route via Stirling where the castle was under English control. By mid-September 1297, the Earl of Surrey was ready to march his men across a bridge over the River Forth beside Stirling Castle though he was very well aware that William Wallace and Andrew Murray were watching from Abbey Craig, a hill on the other side of the river. Surrey had the larger army and was pretty confident that Wallace and Murray would negotiate terms of surrender. They had no intention of doing so – they were determined to fight. The bridge over the River Forth was narrow, so Wallace and Murray waited until a significant part of the English army had crossed before launching their attack. This advance portion of the English army was quickly overwhelmed, and a bloodbath ensued. Surrey recognised that the tables had turned, as he had now lost at least a third of his forces. He ordered that the bridge should be destroyed, leaving his men to their fate on the wrong side. This was quickly followed by an order to retreat. Despite the odds against them, William Wallace and Andrew Murray had defeated the English army at the Battle of Stirling Bridge.

English authority in Scotland collapsed as many Scottish nobles now switched their support to Wallace. This included James Stewart, High Steward of Scotland, who switched sides yet again and followed through by immediately attacking the English baggage train as they retreated. I would like to think someone might have shouted: "Make up your mind, Hamish!" William Wallace and Andrew Murray were appointed joint Guardians of Scotland and would now govern on behalf of their imprisoned king, John Balliol. In keeping with his new status, Wallace was knighted and from this point became Sir William Wallace. Andrew Murray was badly wounded at Stirling and, from what we know, died within two months of the battle, so Wallace would continue alone as the leader of Scotland. It is almost certainly the case that Murray would have been the overall commander at the Battle of Stirling Bridge and without him victory may not have been achieved, but sadly he has become one of Scotland's forgotten heroes. Why he is not properly commemorated is a mystery to me.

Within a few months, Wallace had recaptured many of Scotland's castles and, for the most part, gained the confidence of "fickle" Scottish nobles. Scotland was on the road to freedom from English rule. I wonder how many really believed this though, as after all, they were up against Edward I of England, Hammer of the Scots. Was he simply going to accept the situation? Of course he wasn't. Should we really be surprised that many Scottish nobles were still reluctant to make their support unequivocal? I should mention that the term "Hammer of the Scots" was first used long after Edward's death though I am sure his contemporaries living in Scotland had many other names for him!

By the summer of 1298, an English army was once again marching towards Scotland, led this time by Edward Longshanks himself. Wallace attempted to avoid direct battle with Edward's forces and did everything in his power to destroy their supply chain in the hope they would be forced to retreat. By mid-July, both armies were camped close to Falkirk, so confrontation became unavoidable. What followed at the Battle of Falkirk was by no means a resounding defeat for Wallace but a defeat nonetheless that was undoubtedly assisted by Edward's deployment of his feared archers with their powerful longbows.

Wallace was humiliated and by December had resigned as the Guardian of Scotland. Although he continued to play an active role, including a spell as a diplomat where he travelled in Europe attempting to garner support for Scotland, his glory days were over. To Edward Longshanks though, Wallace was still an enemy who had to be dealt with even if there may have been times when he would have treated him with clemency. However, as time passed, Edward's attitude hardened. By 1305, Wallace also had many enemies among Scottish nobility who considered him to be a troublesome irrelevance, so it became Edward's hope that Wallace might be captured by one of his own countrymen, and as a result, a price remained on his head. On 3 August 1305, Wallace was captured at Robroyston near Glasgow and taken to Dumbarton Castle by Sir John Menteith, who was the Scottish keeper of the castle, appointed by Edward. Sir John would go down in history as the man who betrayed Wallace though some might say he was simply doing his duty. Wallace was taken from there to London and tried for treason despite the fact that he was not, and never had been, an English subject. It was, of course, little more than a show trial, as there was only ever going to be one verdict. He was sentenced to be hung, drawn, and quartered. If they got anything right in the filming of *Braveheart*, it was the brutal portrayal of Wallace's death. It really was that gruesome. His head was displayed on London Bridge and the other four parts of his body were prominently displayed on spikes in Newcastle, Berwick-on-Tweed, Perth, and Stirling Bridge. The latter was doubtless an intended irony. Though the visual effect of this form of execution was obviously a deterrent, there was an added element in that the mutilated body would be denied a Christian burial in consecrated ground, so it was a vengeful punishment that was intended to go beyond the grave.

7

Wars of Independence (Robert The Bruce)

On a cold February day in 1306, two of Scotland's most powerful nobles met at Greyfriars Church in Dumfries. They were John Comyn, Lord of Badenoch, and Robert Bruce, Earl of Carrick. Comyn was the nephew of the deposed John Balliol, and Bruce was the grandson of Robert Bruce, who had been the other main claimant to the Throne of Scotland when, in 1292, Edward I of England had made his choice. Though they had worked together, plotted together, and probably plotted against each other, we will never know for sure why they chose to meet that day. We do know that John Comyn and Robert Bruce both had a strong claim to be King of Scotland and, whether or not by premeditated intent, only one would leave this church alive.

Robert Bruce was the 8th in a long line of Roberts, so in order to keep track, we have to give them numbers. Things would have been so much easier for us today if they had occasionally used other names such as John, Steven, Cedric, Herbert, whatever, but no, they all had to be Robert. The first was a Norman who arrived in England with William the Conqueror in 1066. As a loyal knight, he was awarded a significant area of land in northern England – mainly in Yorkshire. King David I of Scotland had spent part of his youth as an exile in England where, at the English royal court, he had met and became friendly with the 2nd Robert de Brus. When David returned to Scotland, he granted Robert the Lordship of Annandale, so the de Brus family now had a foot in Scotland. The royal connection, leading ultimately to their claim to the Scottish throne, came when the 4th and 5th Robert de Brus both married into the family of William I (the Lion) of Scotland. From that time onward, their family influence in Scotland's affairs increased significantly and continued to do so as each generation passed, though the name would be anglicised to Bruce.

We can safely say that the Bruce family never came to terms with losing their claim to the Scottish throne in 1292 and struggled with the concept of supporting John Balliol as the rightful Scottish monarch, so we should not really be surprised at their occasional divided loyalty. Following Wallace's defeat at Falkirk, when he resigned as the Guardian of Scotland, John Comyn and Robert Bruce were appointed as joint Guardians who would work together in order to govern Scotland on behalf of the imprisoned king, John Balliol. Given their obvious rivalry and the fact that Bruce's family had, for a time, been loyal to Edward of England, this would appear to have been an unusual move. We can only assume that it was intended to foster an element of unity, though realistically, that was never going to last.

In July 1299, Edward agreed to release John Balliol from his imprisonment in the Tower of London on condition that he would retire to his lands in France and play no further part in the governance of Scotland. Though some undoubtedly hoped that Balliol would renege on this commitment, it was never really on the cards. Nevertheless, it still made Bruce uncomfortable, as he had a plan of his own. He had already decided that the Crown of Scotland should not remain with Balliol, nor should it go to any member of the Balliol family. The next King of Scotland would be Bruce himself. He now chose to resign as Guardian of Scotland and made the surprise move of switching his support to Edward I of England. It is easy to be critical of Bruce for his apparent willingness to change sides, but equally, we have to consider the possibility that he was being politically astute and playing the long game. Perhaps the end would justify the means.

Edward Longshanks had failed to completely follow through after his victory at the Battle of Falkirk in 1298, not least because he was yet again caught up with campaigns in France. However, from 1301, further invasions followed till, in 1304, Edward summoned a parliament in England to come up with a plan for a new government in Scotland. This took the form of a council made up of nobles "loyal" to him. Among them were John Comyn and Robert Bruce, so again these two men were working together. Though it is difficult to see how there could have been any form of trust between the main players in this scenario, there is a suggestion that Comyn and Bruce had continued to plot together against the common enemy of Edward Longshanks. Given his now declared loyalty to Edward I of England, Robert Bruce was welcome at the English Court but likely still retained a foot in both camps through an ongoing correspondence with John Comyn. Neither trusted the other, so it is not difficult to believe that

John Comyn may have tried to incriminate Bruce by ensuring that some of that correspondence fell into Edward's hands. When Edward confronted Bruce with the evidence, he was able to convince him that the seal on the letters was either a forgery or had been stolen from him. Bruce knew Edward was not fully satisfied and equally knew he was in danger, so he now fled to Scotland – only hours before Edward's men came to arrest him.

Shortly after came the meeting at Greyfriars Church between Bruce and Comyn. Was this to be a meeting to decide what their next move should be against Edward Longshanks? Was it a "clear the air" meeting to finally decide which of them would claim the Scottish throne, or was it a confrontation about betrayal? Tempers flared, and Bruce drew his dagger and stabbed Comyn. When he left the church, he told his men that he had only wounded Comyn, to which one of Bruce's loyal followers, Sir Roger de Kirkpatrick, replied, "Ise mac siccar" (I will make sure) and then went in the church to indeed make sure – that Comyn was dead. Other versions of how events unfolded are available, of course, so again it has to be said that we will never know the real truth of what happened at Greyfriars Church, or why. There was, however, a certain inevitability about the end result of this feud between Bruce and Comyn, as only one of them could be king.

To murder a fellow noble was one thing but to do so within the sanctity of a church was unforgivable and resulted in Bruce's excommunication by Pope Clement V. Though not a good situation for an aspiring king, he was, nevertheless, crowned at Scone Abbey as Robert I of Scotland a few weeks later. There would be no more switching sides; Bruce had now very publicly chosen his path. It was hardly a great start, as he had not only fallen out with the church but also many of Scotland's nobles, not least the powerful Comyn family. More importantly, he incurred the wrath of Edward I of England by daring to presume himself to be King of Scotland.

Edward Longshanks was in poor health, so he sent his half-cousin Aymer de Valence to Scotland at the head of an army with instructions to "burn, slay, and raise dragon" (the latter part means spare no mercy). Valance was also the brother-in-law of the murdered John Comyn, so this helped him in gaining the active assistance of Comyn's supporters in Scotland. It was not long before Bruce realised that his limited forces were no match for this bolstered English army, so had little choice but to go into hiding. The supporters he left behind were rounded up and dealt with in a brutal manner. His brother Neil was hung, drawn, and quartered. Another two brothers, Thomas and Alexander, would soon suffer the same fate. His wife and daughter were imprisoned and displayed in open cages. Bruce and his family would pay a terrible price for defying Edward Longshanks.

Although, to be honest, we were taught very little Scottish history when I was in school during the 1960s, there is one story relating to the time Robert the Bruce spent in hiding that was commonly told. During the winter of 1306, when seeking refuge in a dark cave somewhere on the Isle of Arran, Bruce was fascinated as he watched a spider trying time and again to build its web on the cave wall. Frequently, the spider would fall, but each time it climbed back up to start again. Bruce was inspired by this and decided there and then that he too had to get up and start again. He had to go back to the fight. Okay, that was first told a few hundred years after Bruce's death, but it is quite likely that the story did inspire a phrase still used in Scotland today. If someone who never gives up when undertaking a difficult task is being praised, you might hear a reaction such as "Aye, lad, you have the heart of Bruce tackling that job." A great compliment to a Scot.

Bruce did return to the mainland in early 1307 and brought a renewed vigour to his campaign. In May, he had defeated a large English force at the Battle of Loudoun Hill and the tide of war began to turn in his direction. By July, Edward I of England was heading north with a large army in order to deal with Bruce once and for all, but this was to be Edward's last campaign. His already failing health took a turn for the worse and Edward I of England, Hammer of the Scots, breathed his last within sight of the Scottish border. His son, now King Edward II, assumed command, but he chose not to fight and turned the army back home. Bruce still had a formidable enemy in England, but he no longer had to deal with Edward Longshanks.

With no obvious sign that Edward II was going to invade, Bruce now had the time he needed to deal with his enemies much closer to home: his enemies in Scotland. He ruthlessly turned his attention to the Comyns and all their supporters. John Comyn, Earl of Buchan (cousin of the murdered John Comyn), was defeated at Inverurie and Bruce then followed through with what came to be known as the "Harrying of Buchan" when farms were burnt, livestock were killed, and any loyal to the Comyns were brutally murdered. He then took control of castles on the north-east coast before heading west towards Duffus, Glen Urquhart, and Inverlochy. Bruce's vengeance was then turned on the Comyn-supporting Macdougalls in Argyll. Destruction of castles was part of Bruce's tactics; if he could not use them, they could not be allowed to remain for someone else to use against him. Bruce was determined to dominate Scotland in a way that Longshanks had tried to do, but ultimately failed. The difference being that Bruce was now becoming recognised as the rightful King of Scotland – even by the church. Well, the Scottish church, at least.

Robert the Bruce had adopted the guerrilla tactics first used by William Wallace and Andrew Murray and this served him well though he knew that a day of reckoning with Edward II had to come. Despite his success, Bruce was nervous and reluctant to commit until a reckless decision by his only surviving brother, Edward Bruce, forced his hand. Stirling Castle was the last major stronghold in Scotland still occupied by English forces under the command of Philip Mowbray. Edward Bruce made a deal with Mowbray that the castle should be surrendered to him without a fight if English reinforcements had not arrived by 24 June 1314, thereby setting the scene for a full-scale confrontation. This also forced the hand of the equally reluctant King Edward II of England, as he now faced the choice of attacking or giving up any claim to Scotland. Edward chose to march an army north to Stirling with himself at its head. The largest army ever to invade Scotland approached Stirling just before the set deadline, but Bruce was already in position and had chosen his ground carefully.

Early on the 23rd of June, the English knight Henry de

Bohun was at the head of a section who were confronted by Scottish spearmen. De Bohun recognised the royal garments worn by the man on horseback organising these Scottish troops and realised it was none other than Robert the Bruce. Seizing the opportunity, he positioned his lance and charged towards the Scottish king. Bruce was by far the more experienced of the two and stood his ground till de Bohun was almost upon him. At the last moment, he stood up in the saddle and swerved to avoid the lance, simultaneously raising his axe to then bring it crashing down on the English knight's head. Henry de Bohun was killed instantly. As this news quickly spread among English troops, it seriously damaged their morale and further boosted the image of Bruce's invincibility. Of course, it was a massive morale booster for the opposing Scottish army. Bruce had expanded on Wallace's idea of schiltrons (large wooden spikes) by constantly drilling his men in a way that allowed them to mobilise the formation, making it an offensive rather than a solely static defensive weapon. Despite being vastly outnumbered, the first day of battle had gone well for Bruce though he was still not convinced that he could win a full-scale set piece battle and was, probably even at this stage, still considering a strategic withdrawal in order to continue with his successful guerrilla war. That night, a Scottish noble, Sir Alexander Seton, who had been fighting on the English side, arrived in the Scots' camp. Though he may have been a defector, it is more likely that he had been a Scottish spy embedded in the English army, but either way, the news he brought would change the course of this battle. He not only brought important information relating to the English army's strategy but was also able to impress upon

Bruce that morale among English troops was at a very low ebb. Bruce made a decision. The next morning, on 24 June 1314, he would launch a full-scale attack. Robert the Bruce may have been outnumbered at the Battle of Bannockburn, but his careful choice of location and superior tactics combined with the ferocious fighting ability of his troops would lead to victory. Edward II fled to Dunbar, where a waiting ship took him safely back to England.

English knights captured at Bannockburn were traded for prisoners who had long been held in England, among them were Bruce's own wife and daughter as well as his friend and mentor Robert Wishart, Bishop of Glasgow. Almost all Scottish nobles, including those who had previously been loyal to the Balliol family, now threw their weight behind Bruce as the undisputed King Robert I of Scotland. Though not the end of the War of Independence, it was certainly the beginning of the end. Bruce had full control of Scotland, so would now concentrate his fight on the north of England. Sooner or later, Edward II would have to fully capitulate.

Robert the Bruce had a lingering problem in that he was still excommunicated by the church in Rome, so in 1320, Scottish nobles decided to write an open letter to Pope John XXII seeking that he recognise Bruce as the rightful King of Scotland. It was drafted by the Abbot of Arbroath Abbey and subsequently came to be known as the Declaration of Arbroath. It also contained something of a "shot across the bow" for Bruce himself or any future Scottish king through a paragraph stating that they reserved the right to turn against any monarch who might acquiesce to English rule. It was the first written document ever to challenge the divine right of kings. Though the full letter was actually pretty long-winded, the most frequently quoted parts are as follows:

> *"As long as but a hundred of us remain alive, never will we on any condition be brought under English rule.*
> *It is not for glory, nor riches, nor honours that we are fighting, but for freedom.*
> *For that alone, which no honest man gives up but with life itself."*

On 6 April 1988, American Senate leader Trent Lott inaugurated the first "Tartan Day" celebration and that included a parade in New York. This was the 668th anniversary of the Declaration of Arbroath and was, of course, a none too subtle attempt to create a Scottish version of St Patrick's Day. Despite having the late, great Sean Connery leading the parade, it was always going to be a pale imitation though it has since evolved into an annual event. Senator Lott is not alone in believing that the wording of the American Declaration of Independence was inspired by the Declaration of Arbroath despite the 450-year gap between the two. Who knows, they may be right. However, I am inclined to think the American Declaration was more heavily influenced by great thinkers from the enlightenment period of the 1700s, and that does include more than a few Scots.

Edward II of England was deposed in 1327 in favour of his son Edward III. Two years later, in 1329, the Treaty of Edinburgh-Northampton was signed between England and

Scotland, guaranteeing "final and perpetual peace" between the two countries. In this year, the Pope finally rescinded the order of excommunication and recognised Bruce as King Robert I of Scotland, the true king of an independent Scotland. It was also the year that Bruce died.

Given the life he led, it is perhaps surprising that he died of natural causes, in his own bed, when he was fifty-four years old. We do not know the cause of death though it is unlikely to have been from leprosy, as has often been stated. Though it is probably true that his father suffered from this dreaded disease, Robert the Bruce could hardly have functioned as a king in the way he did if he too had been afflicted. It is also known that he regularly attended mass, which no leper would have been allowed to do. Confusingly, he was buried in three separate locations, as his internal organs were removed prior to being embalmed and, with the exception of his heart, buried close to his home in Cardross. The embalmed body was then buried in Dunfermline Abbey. Bruce had left instructions that his heart should be taken on a tour of the holy land before being buried at Melrose Abbey, so it was placed in a casket and entrusted to his loyal knight Sir James Douglas. He and his men were diverted to Spain to fight against the Moors, where they came under attack. Knowing he would not survive, Sir James threw the casket forward, shouting, "Lead on, brave heart, I'll follow thee." The body of Sir James Douglas was returned to Scotland, along with the casket. In 1996, during excavation in the ruins of Melrose Abbey, the casket was rediscovered and confirmed as the container that would have conveyed Bruce's heart. It was reburied within the abbey and a plaque now marks the spot.

Now, if you did not already know, you will probably have made the connection between the origin of the term "Braveheart" and the film of that title. It had nothing to do with William Wallace, but everything to do with Robert the Bruce.

It is, of course, a statement of the blindingly obvious that Edward I of England, William Wallace, and Robert the Bruce were men of their time, but it does perhaps give us a bit of leeway when it comes to judging their actions. Tempting though it may be, I am inclined to think that we should avoid making any firm judgement and accept that all three were powerful, driven, brutal men living during brutal times. Of these three men, I think it is fair to say that Bruce was the most complicated, but equally, I think he was the most politically aware and ultimately the most successful. Despite his obvious flaws, I would suggest that Robert the Bruce was the greatest king that Scotland ever had, and certainly not matched by any who came after him.

8

The Bruce Dynasty

Robert the Bruce's only son, David, was crowned King of Scotland upon the death of his father when he was only four years old. Not for the first or the last time, regents would rule on behalf of a very young monarch. Despite his tender years, he was already married to Joanna, the daughter of England's King Edward II, as per terms written into the Treaty of Northampton though the "final and perpetual peace" referred to in that treaty did not last long. Three years, to be exact.

In 1327 (two years before the death of Bruce), Edward II of England had been deposed. Again, I must briefly mention the film *Braveheart* in relation to the sexuality of King Edward II. Yes, he was probably homosexual, but it was more his choice of male lovers that would lead to his downfall. Hugh le Despenser, son of the Earl of Winchester, was very close to the King, but he was also a tyrant who abused his position to the extent that he became one of the most feared nobles in England and Wales. Edward did nothing to control Despenser and continued the relationship. The inevitable rebellion, when it came, was led by the King's own wife, Isabella, and her accomplice, Roger Mortimer, 1st Earl of March. When captured, Hugh le Despenser was hung, drawn, and quartered. As for Edward, he was imprisoned in Berkeley Castle after having first been "persuaded" to abdicate in favour of his fourteen-year-old son, who became Edward III. He was never seen again and died later that year. Legend has it that he was killed by having a red-hot poker thrust into his rear. Major fallouts among members of the royal family are nothing new, though fortunately, our current royals do not resort to such extremes. Their main weapon today is more likely to be a carefully targeted media leak.

Just three years later, young Edward III gained full control of his own kingdom and immediately had Mortimer executed and his mother removed from the royal court. His father's death had been avenged. Though Edward II had, without question, been one of England's worst kings, Edward III was more in the mould of his grandfather (Edward Longshanks) and probably looked upon Scotland as unfinished business. He secretly supported the claim of John Balliol's son Edward over that of Bruce's son David. Edward Balliol pledged to return Berwick-on-Tweed (it had been recaptured by Bruce) to England if he became king, providing he received military assistance from Edward III. It was too tempting an offer for Edward, who now marched an army north to Berwick where, in July 1333, he defeated Scottish forces at the Battle of Halidon Hill. For their safety, young David II of Scotland and his bride were exiled in France, and seven years would pass before his supporters in Scotland achieved the required stability for their return. This more than likely became possible due to Edward being otherwise occupied with his increasing commitment to war with France.

Upon his return in 1341, David took direct control of his kingdom and shortly after went to war with England in support of the French – as per "the Auld Alliance". Unfortunately for David, he was captured at the Battle of Neville's Cross in 1346 and spent the next eleven years as a prisoner in England. I say prisoner, but it was really a comfortable existence in both Odiham Castle and Windsor Castle. Edward III was his brother-in-law and, for once, it would appear that family relations worked in his favour. David felt that Windsor Castle could do with a little upgrading and apparently suggested that the money could be raised by a ransom for his own release. Though negotiations went on for some time, Scotland did eventually agree to pay England the equivalent of almost £70,000 for the return of their king. In Berwick (where else), the deal was signed. The ransom would be paid in instalments, and David II was free to return to Scotland though by then he had also agreed to accept Edward III of England as his feudal overlord. After everything his father had fought for, it seemed that Scotland was already slipping back to where they had started.

Since David had returned to a country that was stricken with poverty, there was very little chance that the ransom money could be paid, so he now chose to make a deal with Edward that would, upon his death, mean passing the throne of Scotland to the English king or one of his sons. In return, the debt would be cancelled. Much to David's annoyance, Scottish nobles dismissed this completely and chose to pay the debt, however long it took. He was very fortunate that only a few of these nobles came out strongly against him by invoking the Declaration of Arbroath, resulting in a relatively small rebellion that he was quickly able to put down. The burden of this ransom payment imposed high taxes on an already fragile Scottish economy, which inevitably caused tensions and was not helped by a suspicion that David II was frequently retaining a large slice of the income for his own personal benefit rather than making the due payments. He died with no heir in 1371, and one suspects there were very few who mourned his passing. Had it not been for David's enforced absence from his kingdom, things may have been different, but the truth is that the Bruce dynasty consisted of one great king and one who, at best, has to be described as less than great!

9

The Stewart Dynasty

Robert II and Robert III

David II was succeeded by his nephew, who became Robert II. He was the son of Robert the Bruce's daughter Marjory, who had married Walter, the 6th High Steward of Scotland, resulting in a new royal house – the House of Stewart. The very first High Steward was appointed in 1157 and it subsequently became a hereditary title. Officially, the Steward controlled the domestic affairs of the royal household, so it evolved into a high-ranking position that allowed the 6th High Steward to marry into the royal family. Though the House of Bruce only lasted for thirty-five years, there would be almost 350 years between the crowning of the first and the death of the last monarch from the House of Stewart.

Robert the Bruce's grandson was fifty-four years old when he became Robert II of Scotland and already had considerable experience in governing the country, as he had been regent during his uncle's long periods of absence, and yes, Robert was eight years older than his uncle David. The reign of David II had hardly been a great success, but maybe Robert II would be more like his illustrious grandfather? No, as it turns out, he definitely would not. Even Robert himself seemed to acknowledge that he was no longer up to the job, as he effectively transferred power to his oldest son John Stewart, the Earl of Carrick. Unfortunately for John, he suffered serious injury when kicked by a horse, so Robert II replaced him as regent with his second son, Robert Stewart, Duke of Albany.

By the time Robert II died in 1390, John had sufficiently recovered from his injuries to take up his rightful place as heir to the throne. Yet again we have the added confusion of too many Bruces/Stewarts sharing the same name, as John now changed his name to guess what? Yes, that's right, he chose to reign as "Robert" III. In fairness, we have to accept that John was probably not the best name for a Stuart king at that time, as it was a very obvious reminder of their rival, John Balliol. As you can imagine, this did not go down very well with his younger brother who had enjoyed the power of being regent, not to mention the fact his name actually was Robert. Another brother, Alexander Stewart, terrorised the people of the Highlands from his lair at Lochindorb Castle in Badenoch, where he owned vast areas of land granted to him by his father; land that had mostly been taken from the Comyns. His marriage to the Countess of Ross produced no children, so he sought an annulment, but the Bishop of Moray refused and instead had Alexander excommunicated. He took his revenge by burning nearby towns and churches, including Elgin Cathedral. The law was on his side simply because, in that area, he was the law, so it is little wonder that he came to be known as the "Wolf of Badenoch". The story of his death in 1394 tells of a tall dark man who visited Alexander one night when he was staying at

Ruthven Castle, beside Kingussie (now the ruin of Ruthven Barracks). All through the night, the stranger and Alexander played chess till shortly before dawn when a sudden violent storm shook the very foundations of the castle and the visitor shouted over the deafening noise: "Check, and checkmate." When daylight appeared, the visitor had gone and the body of the Wolf of Badenoch was found, stretched out on the high table in the banqueting hall. And the moral of the story is – don't play chess with the devil.

Robert III, who now took the throne, was certainly the eldest son of Robert II, but there was a question about his legitimacy, as his parents were not actually married till after his birth. Add in his continuing ill health following his accident, and it quickly becomes obvious that he was not in a strong position. He was also seriously undermined by his younger brother Robert, Duke of Albany, who never fully relinquished power after having been regent. By 1398, the King's health was of such concern that senior nobles appointed his son David, 1st Duke of Rothesay, to rule on his behalf. However, his uncle Robert (Albany) used what power he still had to arrest, or I should really say kidnap, the twenty-four-year-old David and had him imprisoned in Falkland Palace, where he was literally starved to death. Robert III was now anxious to protect his youngest son, James Stewart, and arranged for him to go into hiding. Unfortunately, that did not work out too well, as the ship taking young James overseas was attacked by pirates who then chose to hand their prize capture over to Scotland's enemy, Henry IV of England. Robert was at Rothesay Castle on the Isle of Bute when he was told of his son's capture and died shortly after. Robert III of Scotland wrote his own epitaph and clearly thought as much of himself as everyone else did.

> *"Let those men who strive in this world for the pleasures of honour have shining monuments. I on the other hand should prefer to be buried at the bottom of a midden, so that my soul may be saved on the day of the lord.*
>
> *Bury me therefore, I beg you, in a midden, and write for my epitaph: Here lies the worst of kings and the most wretched of men in the whole kingdom."*

He was, in fact, buried at Paisley Abbey – unworthy of being buried at Scone Abbey alongside other kings. It is incredible to think that such a weak, deceitful, treacherous line of royal brothers could come from the great King Robert the Bruce, but they did. And nowadays William and Harry think they have problems!

James I

Robert III's twelve-year-old son now became James I, the rightful King of Scotland, even if he was a "prisoner" at the court of England's Henry IV and would not return to Scotland for another eighteen years. In the meantime, his uncle Robert, Duke of Albany, ruled as regent and made little or no attempt to negotiate his nephew's release, as he had nothing to gain from this but had a great deal to lose. Somehow though, he found the time to negotiate the release of his own son, Murdoch Stewart, who had also been held captive in England. It is fair to say that

James actually benefited from his long period in England, as he was not only treated throughout with dignity, but Henry IV ensured that he also received a good education. Having spent all of his formative years at the English Court, we should not be surprised that James came to respect Henry and, at one point, even joined him on a campaign against France. That, as you can imagine, did not go down too well in his homeland, as Scottish forces were fighting in France at that time against England.

In February 1424, James, now in his late twenties, was married to Lady Joan Beaufort, daughter of the Earl of Somerset and a half-cousin of King Henry IV. Following the marriage, serious negotiations, now instigated by Henry, finally got underway for his release in order that he could take his rightful place as King James I of Scotland. Three months after their wedding, James returned to Scotland with his queen Joan. His uncle Robert, Duke of Albany, had died four years earlier, but this did not stop James from exacting revenge. All close family members of the late duke were imprisoned or executed, including James's cousin Murdoch who had inherited the title of the Duke of Albany. James I of Scotland was now in charge and determined to put into practice all that he had learned from his mentor Henry IV of England. His reforming zeal in the areas of finance and law probably stemmed from his English education and certainly helped to modernise procedures in Scotland, but given the corrupt governance experienced under his uncle, it is hardly surprising that he would face mounting opposition. Certain Scottish nobles were going to do whatever it took to undermine James I and would now revive the question over his father's, and therefore his, legitimacy in order to justify their position, but James was no shrinking violet and had proved this by the ruthless way he had dealt with his Albany relatives. Although his only surviving uncle, Walter Stewart, the Earl of Atholl, was a potential rival, he initially appeared to be loyal to James. Walter had played a significant part during negotiations for his release from English captivity and he had been a member of the jury that tried and executed members of the Albany family. James trusted Walter Stewart and even appointed him to the position of Great Justiciar of Scotland, effectively putting him in charge of governing the country. He also appointed Walter's grandson Robert Stewart as his personal chamberlain. This was another important position very close to the King. Was James naive to trust any member of his own family? Yes, of course he was. Whether it had been part of Walter's plan all along or something happened that changed his mind we will never know, but Walter now plotted against James in order to take the throne of Scotland for himself and thereafter his line of the Stewart family.

On 20 February 1437, James and his court were staying at Blackfriars Priory in Perth. That evening, the King was relaxing in his chambers in the company of his queen and her ladies in waiting when they all heard a commotion outside. They immediately sensed they were in danger. James's personal chamberlain, Robert Stewart, had opened the gates and allowed entry to a group of around thirty conspirators who were determined to assassinate the King. The traitorous chamberlain had disabled internal door locks, so one of the ladies, Catherine Douglas, used her arm to bar the door while the King pulled up floorboards in an attempt to escape through the drain passage beneath. The attackers very quickly forced their way through to the King's inner chamber, breaking Catherine's arm in the process and giving us the legendary figure of "Kate Barlass" (the heroic lass who barred the door). Tragically for James, her efforts were in vain, as the assassins caught up with him and the King was brutally murdered. Apparently, his love of tennis may have contributed to his death. Too many balls bounced from the tennis court into a nearby open drain, so he had it blocked up to prevent more balls being lost, thereby also blocking his only escape route. Advantage assassins.

James II

Though injured, the Queen was somehow, in the middle of this confusion, able to escape to the safety of Stirling Castle. Her six-year-old son who, due to a facial birth mark, came to be known as "James of the fiery face" was now King James II of Scotland. Fortunately for him, he also had a fiery mother who immediately sought revenge on the Stewart side of the family responsible for the murder of his father. Whilst it is true that some within Scottish nobility would not have mourned the death of James I, there was very little support for the murderous action taken by Walter Stewart, so the conspirators were soon taken prisoner, and all were executed in a truly barbaric manner. As the ringleader, Walter Stewart, Earl of Atholl, was to suffer the most. He was tortured for three days before he could welcome the mercy of exhaling his final breath.

James II was not crowned at Scone Abbey as previous kings but was instead the first to be crowned at Holyrood Abbey. The coronation took place in March 1437, two months after his father's death, though, of course, others would rule on his behalf until such time as he came of age. Had it not been the case that so many Scottish kings were crowned when they were juveniles, it is just about possible that we may have had at least one or two successful Stewart monarchs though I admit that may be slightly fanciful. It might at least have prevented the country from so frequently having to be governed by self-serving, treacherous regents. That, of course, is not how it worked out and young James II was to become yet another pawn between rival noble families. Queen Joan, his mother, initially became joint regent alongside the King's first cousin Archibald, 5th Earl of Douglas. Following the death of Archibald, who had been a weak and ineffectual leader, lesser nobles William Crichton, Lord Chancellor of Scotland, and Sir Alexander Livingston of Callander seized control. They briefly placed the Queen and her new husband, the Douglas-supporting Sir James Stewart, under arrest and forced her to give up custody of her son. Though Crichton and Livingston had an uneasy relationship, they shared a strong desire to prevent any future Douglas family influence. On 24 November 1440, they invited the sixteen-year-old William, 6th Earl of Douglas, and his eleven-year-old brother David, accompanied by their friend Sir Malcolm Fleming of Cumbernauld, to a conciliatory dinner with King James at Edinburgh Castle. By all accounts, the now ten-year-old king enjoyed the company of the Douglas brothers who were, after all, only slightly older than himself, so the dinner was going well. At the end of the meal, proceedings took a very dark turn when a black bull's head was brought in and placed in the centre of the table. This was traditionally a sign of impending death for the chief guests. Despite James's pleas for the lives of his newfound friends to be spared, all three were charged with treason, pronounced guilty, and summarily executed in front of the distraught young king. It came to be known as the "Black Dinner". Heaven forbid that chroniclers of the period might have embellished the story, but either way, the fact remains that even by the treacherous standards of the time, this was a particularly evil act. You might be surprised to hear that the uncle of the 6th Earl of Douglas, who now inherited the title and Douglas estates, may have actually connived in his nephew's execution. No, perhaps by now you might not.

Following his marriage in 1449 to the fifteen-year-old Mary of Guelders, nineteen-year-old James assumed active control as James II of Scotland. Though he took revenge on the Livingstons by removing them from power, he was unable to govern without the assistance and cooperation of the Douglas family despite his suspicion that they were forging links with others, such as John Macdonald, Lord of the Isles, whose loyalty to the King may have been suspect, to say the least. This came to a head on 22 February 1452 when James invited the 8th Earl of Douglas to dine with him at Stirling Castle. Remembering the "Black Dinner", the Earl demanded safe passage, which the King assured him of, though in reality, he probably had little choice but to attend. Needless to say, an argument started, and tempers flared. The King lost control and, in a fit of blind rage, stabbed the Earl of Douglas no fewer than twenty-six times before having his body thrown, unceremoniously, out of the castle window. This, of course, was not the end of his problems with the Douglas family, as the struggle would continue for a few more years before James finally gained the upper hand. The more peaceful period that followed allowed him to govern more freely and to come up with very important decrees, such as the banning of that strange game where people walk around a field carrying a stick and try to put a small ball in little holes in the ground. Too many of James's subjects were wasting time on this silly game when they should instead be practising archery.

In 1460, James turned his attention to regaining control of Roxburgh Castle, as it was the only one in Scotland still under English control. Due to his interest in artillery, he took personal control of the siege and chose to use a number of new cannons he had recently acquired. He was standing beside one of these large cannons, which he had chosen to fire in honour of the arrival of his queen, when it exploded. The King suffered serious injury and died a few hours later. He was only twenty-nine years old. James II was the first king to be buried at Holyrood Abbey as, indeed, he had been the first king crowned there. "Groundhog Day" springs to mind when we talk about Stewart monarchs, as patterns keep repeating. It was certainly the case with James II and his son James III, as their early lives were strikingly similar.

James III

Following the accidental death of James II, his nine-year-old son was immediately crowned James III in Kelso Abbey. His mother, Queen Mary, initially acted as regent though once again a young Scottish king would become a pawn among his "loyal" nobles. In his case, it would mainly be the Boyds of Kilmarnock who would attempt to gain control over him though they must have been aware that their charge would, in the customary manner, turn against them when he came of age. That duly happened in 1468. The following year, as a young adult, James III of Scotland married Margaret of Denmark, daughter of Kristian I, who was king of Norway, Denmark, and Sweden. As part of the marriage settlement, Scotland was to receive a dowry of 80,000 guilders to be paid in instalments, with the Orkney and Shetland Isles being put up as collateral. Unfortunately for King Kristian, the debt could not be settled, so ownership of these islands was transferred to Scotland. To some extent, this formalised a situation that had already been heading in that general direction since 1379 when Henry Sinclair of Roslin had been appointed as the Earl of Orkney. James III had "inadvertently" expanded Scottish territory through the simple act of marriage.

James III was not a popular king, as he had an unfortunate habit of ignoring his senior and most powerful nobles in favour of lesser nobility he personally preferred. Though laudable in some respects, it was not the actions of a wise king if he wanted to retain his power, and it undoubtedly left him open to frequent, and probably justifiable, accusations of corruption. It almost goes without saying that in typical Stewart fashion, his brothers Alexander Stewart, the Duke of Albany, and John Stewart, the Earl of Mar, turned against him, so James had them tried for treason. Though Alexander went into exile in England, John was imprisoned in Craigmillar Castle near Edinburgh and shortly after died in mysterious circumstances.

However, Alexander returned to Scotland in 1482, this

time along with an English army after having made a pact with Edward IV of England that would have put him, rather than his brother James, on the Scottish throne. James raised an army but once again ignored his most able nobles and instead put his favourites in command with the inevitable result that he would now face a domestic rebellion as well as an English invasion. For some reason, probably inadequate funds, the English did not follow through on their invasion, though the Town of Berwick-on-Tweed was taken by English forces and, in the process, changed hands for the thirteenth and final time. Given the confused situation with James's brother who, with English support, was trying to take the Scottish Crown, and the internal rebellion by Scottish nobles, it is hardly surprising that it would end without any real conclusion. Though initially taken prisoner, James III was released and resumed control.

Now you really would think that a king who came so close to losing his kingdom would have thought carefully about the path he would take from then on, but no, not James III; he simply carried on as before. By 1488, he faced another revolt, but this time he even had his own fifteen-year-old son, who had fallen under the influence of rebel nobles, turn against him. I know you will be surprised to hear that the son (his oldest) was another James! This rebellion came to an end when the King's army met the rebel forces at Sauchieburn, which is close to Stirling and very near to the site of the Battle of Bannockburn, where Bruce had won his famous victory many years before. It has even been suggested that James III carried Bruce's original sword into battle that day, though if true, it ultimately did nothing to help him. Loyalist forces were defeated and James, who had been seriously wounded in the conflict, died shortly afterwards. He was buried at Cambuskenneth Abbey and his fifteen-year-old son, who had been the figurehead for the rebellion, was crowned as James IV of Scotland.

James IV

We do not know why, but it is clear that James III appeared to favour his younger son, so his older son, and heir, may have feared for his position in the line of succession. Though that may well have influenced young James's decision to support the rebellion in 1488, it is very unlikely that he would have expected it to result in his father's death and there is no evidence to suggest his active participation in that event. We do know that he carried a heavy guilt and chose to wear a heavy iron chain round his waist for the rest of his life as a penance for the part he did play.

Many of our touring guests are surprised to learn about the chaotic reign of many early Stewart monarchs, and from our conversations, the reality of that period clearly does not sit well with pre-conceived ideas they may have had about Scotland's "heroic struggle" with their enemy in England. In truth, the real enemy was frequently much closer to home and, as you will have gathered by now, too many Scottish monarchs of that period suffered from the problem of "second son syndrome". Yes, conflict with England was never far away, but it is also fair to add that too many early Stewarts were their own worst enemies.

Despite his dubious beginning, James IV was arguably to become one of the most successful Stewart monarchs though up to that point it is fair to say that he had zero competition. James was an intelligent and politically astute young man who immediately assumed control of his kingdom and firmly established his authority. This was a king who would take a "hands on" approach to the governance of his country and clearly recognised that he had to be one step ahead of any who might rebel against him. John Macdonald, Lord of the Isles, who had openly signed a treaty of mutual assistance with England's Edward IV, was one such threat. In 1493, James took decisive action against the Macdonald chief by removing his title and hereditary rights over the Hebridean Islands. He then bestowed the title on himself, thereby ensuring that the King of Scotland would now be the sole authority throughout the Western Isles. His ability to speak several languages was a definite advantage and helped him to control and govern all parts of his kingdom. The fact that he was directly involved in setting up Scotland's first printing press tells us that he was a forward-thinking king who was aware of the benefits of communication. James IV took a great interest in the arts, science, medicine (he founded the Edinburgh Royal College of Surgeons) and is generally looked upon as a modern man of his time. He also sought to strengthen Scotland militarily by creating two naval dockyards, giving the country its first significant naval force.

Scotland's uneasy relationship with England improved in 1503 when James IV of Scotland married Margaret Tudor, daughter of England's King Henry VII and, of course, sister to the future Henry VIII. This was the result of another Treaty of Perpetual Peace between the two countries though you cannot help thinking that, when writing the word "perpetual", the signatories must have had one hand on the pen whilst tightly crossing their fingers on the other. It would take another hundred years, but this marriage would ultimately change the course of history for Scotland and England.

By 1513, Henry VIII was the King of England and that year he chose to take his country to war with France. Although he was entering a European conflict (War of the League of Cambrai) that was primarily focused on Italy, Henry VIII was never one to miss an opportunity that might extend his territory and influence, but in doing so, he gave James IV a problem. Should he stay out of it and passively support his brother-in-law Henry, as per the Treaty of Perpetual Peace, or should he fulfil his obligations under the terms of the Auld Alliance and actively support the French? In fairness to James IV, it has to be noted that Henry VIII had already ignored the Treaty of Perpetual Peace by openly declaring that he did not consider the Scottish king to be his equal and still looked upon himself as James's "overlord", so fully expected his unquestioning loyalty and support. Could this have influenced the Scottish king's decision? I think the answer may be yes. Whatever his motives, James IV opted to stand by the Auld Alliance and supported France.

In early August 1513, an estimated 30,000, possibly up to 40,000, Scottish troops marched out towards England with James IV at their head and almost all of Scotland's senior nobles at his side. This was the largest Scots army ever to go into battle, so initially at least, confidence was high. However, there were many nobles who questioned the need for this action and Queen

Margaret – bear in mind that she was Henry VIII's sister – implored her husband not to proceed. On 9 September 1513, they were confronted on Flodden Field (Branxton Moor), close to the border, though by now the numbers had been significantly depleted through desertion among the ranks. We cannot be sure of the actual number, but it was perhaps around 25,000 Scots lined up against a similar number of English troops under the experienced command of the Earl of Surrey. By this time, morale had dropped, as many in James's army, including senior nobles, felt that a full-scale conflict was an unnecessary danger. A popular king he may have been, but he was a typical Stewart and would not take advice – he knew best! Though they may have initially chosen their ground well, this was not matched by their discipline, so any advantage was soon lost. They were also hampered by the choice of a long, unwieldy pike as their main weapon, not to mention the fact that they had not been fully trained in its use. It was, in any case, pretty useless in the ensuing hand-to-hand combat compared to the shorter bill hook (a type of bladed hook) used by English troops. The centre of the battle turned into a killing field where up to 10,000 Scots died in the space of a few hours, compared to around 1,500 on the English side. Most of Scotland's senior nobles perished along with their king. The reign of James IV had brought in a new type of Stewart monarch who had mostly been held in high esteem, but it ended with the worst ever defeat in Scotland's history. As if to enforce this defeat, we do not know where, or even if, James's body was buried. We do know that it was taken to London and stored for many years in Sheen Priory in Surrey, with Henry VIII initially refusing burial on the grounds that James IV had been excommunicated by the church so could not be buried in consecrated ground, though in truth, that excommunication had been no more than revenge for his decision to support France. Henry VIII did, apparently, later receive papal permission for burial, but there is no record to say it actually happened. For those who like conspiracy theories, there is a possible question as to whether or not that was the actual body of James IV. Yes, the remains taken to London had been clothed in royal garments but not the "penance chain" he had worn every day since he was fifteen years old – it was never found. By all accounts, the head had at some point become detached from the body and some say it was buried under a pub that was supposedly called the "Red Herring". Wherever the remains of King James IV of Scotland lie, it was an exceptionally undignified end for someone who could have been a great king.

There is a bagpipe tune (also a poem and a song) called 'The Flowers of the Forest' that you would recognise, even if the name is not familiar, as it is frequently played at poignant events such as remembrance services. Now, I enjoy the powerful sound of a mass pipe band, but despite being a proud Scot, I have to admit that I really struggle when it comes to a lone piper. When I hear that sound, I tend to look around to see who accidentally stood on a cat.

But, even for me, there are exceptions. A number of years ago, I was at Flodden with a Canadian family by the name of Mackenzie who wanted to scatter the ashes of their father/grandfather in that area. This was a very personal moment, so I pointed them towards an area I thought would be appropriate and left them alone. Though there are rolling hills around

Flodden, it is a fairly open space with large fields, so you can see and hear for quite a distance. It is a beautiful and peaceful place nowadays, but on that warm summer's day, it felt even quieter than normal with only the occasional sound of a buzzing insect to break the silence. The family's travel agent had arranged for a piper to play throughout as the ashes were being scattered and he chose to position himself on the slightly elevated position close to the Flodden Monument. As I watched the family from a distance, I heard the strains of 'The Flowers of the Forest' drifting across and immediately felt a sudden but immensely powerful wave of emotion surge through me. I remember the feeling of relief that I was alone as my eyes began to fill with tears that were soon rolling down my cheeks. Believe me, such a reaction took me completely by surprise, as I had no inkling that I would feel this way until I heard the first few notes being played. It may have been connected to the fact that my own maternal grandfather was a Mackenzie, who died long before I was born, or it could simply have been the location, but I truthfully do not know. I still believe that bagpipes can produce truly awful sounds, but there are times when even I have to admit they can produce raw emotion so strong that, if you do not feel it, you are already dead, and nobody has told you.

James V

Scotland's next king, another James you will doubtless be surprised to hear, was less than two years old when his father was killed at Flodden. On 21 September 1513, he was taken by his mother from their residence at Linlithgow Palace to Stirling Castle where, in the Chapel Royal, he was crowned as James V of Scotland. In the very familiar pattern we have come to recognise, the young James's mother, Margaret Tudor, was appointed as regent. Given that she was the sister of Henry VIII, it is hardly surprising that many Scottish nobles (of those left after Flodden) were very suspicious of Margaret, so a year later, following her marriage to Archibald Douglas, 6th Earl of Angus, she was replaced by the King's uncle, John Stewart, 2nd Duke of Albany. Again, this all sounds very familiar though it has to be said that the Duke of Albany appears to have spent ten successful years in that position before returning to his home in France. By this time, Margaret Tudor had separated from the Earl of Douglas and returned to the position as regent for her son though it is worth mentioning that her marriage to the Earl did produce one child, Lady Margaret, who would in due course marry Mathew Stewart, the Earl of Lennox. Their son, Lord Darnley, would play a very significant role within a future generation of Stewarts. Perhaps as an act of revenge against his wife and with a likely eye to the future, Archibald Douglas kidnapped young James and held him captive for almost three years. Though James was probably treated well during this time, he felt nothing but contempt for his stepfather and finally escaped from him in 1528. He was only fourteen years old but James now assumed control as monarch and, surprise, surprise, his first act was to outlaw his hated stepfamily who were left with no choice but to flee into exile. By all accounts, James was highly strung and prone to showing his emotions, but he did establish his authority and gained popularity with ordinary citizens, as he would frequently go among them in disguise to find out how they really lived.

In 1537, James was married to Madeleine de Valois, daughter of King Francis of France. This brought a substantial dowry to the Scottish king, but sadly Madeleine died within months of the wedding. The following year, he married another French lady of noble birth, Mary of Guise, who had previously, and wisely, turned down a marriage proposal from England's King Henry VIII. Although the Reformation was spreading throughout Europe, James remained firmly within the Catholic faith and was certainly not averse to burning the occasional "heretic". As we all know, Henry VIII departed from the Church of Rome and put himself at the head of the "Church of England" and then grew increasingly annoyed that his nephew, James V of Scotland, would not follow his lead. Relations between the two monarchs deteriorated even more following the death of James's mother, Margaret Tudor, as he then felt free of any allegiance to England. In 1541, Henry invited James to a conference in the town of York in an apparent attempt to resolve their differences, but James was suspicious of his uncle's motives and decided not to attend. Henry VIII had been snubbed and, as you can imagine, that went down badly; so badly that Henry began to mobilise his forces.

Once again, Scotland and England were at war. Though the Scots won an early victory in August 1542 at the Battle of Haddon Rig, near the border, they suffered a crushing defeat at the Battle of Solway Moss just two months later. James had fought with his troops on previous occasions but he was struck by illness and, subsequently, retreated to Falkland Palace to recuperate. He was devastated by the defeat at Solway and now eagerly awaited news from Linlithgow Palace about his heavily pregnant queen. On 8 December 1542, Mary de Guise gave birth to a daughter, Mary Stewart, who was now the sole heir to the Scottish throne. James's condition deteriorated and, on the 15th of December, he passed away. Among his last recorded words were, "It came wi a lass, it'll gang wi a lass." In other words, the Stewart dynasty came through the daughter of Robert the Bruce and would end with his daughter. Ultimately, his prophecy was accurate, but the end would not actually come with his daughter, Mary Queen of Scots.

10

Mary Queen of Scots

Mary Stewart became Queen of Scotland within six days of her birth and was to become the most controversial of all Scottish monarchs. Most of our guests are familiar with her story though again it can often be through fictionalised versions of her life as portrayed on cinema and television screens. However, we are fortunate that many historians have studied the life and times of Mary Queen of Scots in great detail, so we have the information available to help us to form our own opinion about who she was and how her decisions affected the politics of her time. Even allowing for this wealth of information, we can struggle at times, as expert opinion can be even more divided than normal when it comes to Mary Queen of Scots. Was she a frivolous, self-centred, out of touch monarch who made a series of bad decisions, or was she simply the wrong person, in the wrong place, at the wrong time?

Mary was the great-granddaughter of England's King Henry VII and a niece of Henry VIII, who, as you might recall, divorced his first wife, Catherine of Aragon, against the wishes of the Catholic Church. In the eyes of the church, Henry's children from future marriages would be classed as illegitimate, so the young Mary Stewart, as well as being Queen of Scotland, was seen by many as the only true heir to the English throne. Henry's answer was to arrange a marriage between Mary and his son Edward, who was only five years older than the Scottish queen. A treaty was drawn up, stating that Mary would be betrothed to Edward by her tenth birthday, but most of Scotland's nobles refused to have it ratified, not least because Henry was obviously determined to use this as a means of ending Scotland's Auld Alliance with France and forcing his own authority on the country. What followed was much later dubbed the "Rough Wooing". This term, first used by Sir Walter Scott, is a good description, as Henry VIII launched a series of attacks against Scotland that continued after his death in 1547 – his English nobles were equally determined that young Mary and Edward should marry. Scottish nobles continued to resist, as acceptance would also mean having to adopt the English Reformation and becoming a Protestant country at a time when Scotland was still loyal to the Pope. Later that year, the Duke of Somerset, acting on behalf of Henry's young son David, launched a major attack aimed at forcing the Scots to finally agree to this marriage that would unify the Crowns of Scotland and England. The Scots were heavily defeated close to Edinburgh at the Battle of Pinkie Cleugh, which has got to be the most ridiculous name for any battle ever fought in Scotland since the literal translation would come out as "Battle of the small finger narrow valley"!

At the invitation of Henri II of France, young Mary was taken to the safety of the French royal court, where she would stay till she was eighteen years old. Mary was now to marry the

French king's son Francis, Dauphin of France, so once again, Scotland chose France over their English neighbours. As they grew up together, it is clear that Mary was very fond of Francis and treated him like a younger brother, but Francis was generally a sickly child and suffered from deformities that prevented him from fully maturing, so it did not bode well for their future life together. However, at the age of fifteen, Mary was formally married to the fourteen-year-old Dauphin in a very grand ceremony at Notre Dame Cathedral though it appears to have been common knowledge that his condition would have prevented consummation of the marriage, so the relationship they had as children probably changed very little. Her father-in-law, Henri II, now declared Mary to be the rightful heir to the English throne. Although he eventually acknowledged Elizabeth I as England's reigning monarch, he insisted that Mary should be officially declared as the heir to Elizabeth; a position supported by most Catholics throughout Europe. Henri II of France died in July 1559 from injuries sustained in a joust, and the Dauphin and his wife Mary became King and Queen of France. Mary was now Queen of Scotland, Queen of France, and seen by many as heir to the throne of England. At sixteen years old, Mary was potentially the most powerful monarch in Europe, but this was not to last, as the young King Francis died in December of 1560. Mary was no longer the Queen of France, no longer had the support of her powerful mother-in-law (Catherine de Medici), and quickly realised she was no longer needed, or wanted, in France. In 1561, Mary Queen of Scots reluctantly returned to her home country.

On 19 August 1561, a small fleet of Scottish ships, under

the command of the Earl of Bothwell (who will crop up again), sailed into the Port of Leith with Scotland's queen. They arrived earlier than expected, so had to wait for the arrival of Mary's illegitimate half-brother James Stewart, Earl of Moray, who would escort her to Holyrood Palace. A good-sized crowd had turned out to meet their queen and all were impressed by the tall, graceful, cheerful young lady they came to see. A banquet was held in her honour that night and loud celebrations could be heard throughout the city.

Mary was, of course, Scottish and spoke the language fluently (albeit with a strong French accent), but she had lived at the French royal court since she was five years old, so it is hardly surprising that she would now model her Scottish court along French lines. The French spelling of her name, Stuart, was adopted from a young age and all those within her family started to use that spelling to show support for their queen. Most of her household servants had come with her from France, so they too were used to a glamorous lifestyle that simply did not exist in Scotland. The contrast for Mary could not have been greater and she struggled to understand why so many of her subjects were starting to look upon her court as frivolous; to some, her lifestyle was outright offensive.

The country that defied Henry VIII by refusing to allow his son to marry the very young Mary and embrace the English Reformation had by now done a complete turnaround. Scotland had not simply embraced the Reformation, no, they had gone much further than England by adopting the more rigid Calvinist ideas and established the Presbyterian movement. This was led by John Knox, who famously wrote a pamphlet entitled 'The First Blast of the Trumpet Against the Monstrous Regiment of Women'. John Knox was adamant that a female in any position of power was an abomination, so you can guess that he did not approve of Mary as a ruling monarch. Elizabeth I of England may have been a fellow Protestant but was, to say the least, highly offended by Knox's teaching and banished him from England. Mary, on the other hand, was a Catholic queen in a country that was immersed in Presbyterianism, so Knox felt more secure at home in Scotland and verbally attacked Mary at every opportunity. His attacks continued even though Mary had made it clear that, as long as she could continue to practise her faith in the way she chose, she would rule in a way that did not discriminate. I think it is fair to say that she genuinely intended that all Scots, Catholic or Protestant, would be free to worship without fear of intolerance, but this was never going to be enough for John Knox, who wanted a Protestant monarch – ideally a king.

It has often been suggested that Elizabeth I of England chose not to marry as it would inevitably mean ceding power to a husband who would become a king, but that did not appear to concern Mary, her cousin and fellow queen. A number of European princes and senior nobles were put forward, with Queen Elizabeth even suggesting her own favourite, the Earl of Leicester. Rather than enter a politically suitable marriage, Mary put her own feelings first and fell for her handsome young cousin, Lord Darnley. On 29 July 1565, Mary Queen of Scots, who by now was twenty-three years old, married the nineteen-year-old Henry Stewart, Lord Darnley. They shared the same grandmother (Margaret Tudor), so it was the belief of many Catholics that, after Mary, Darnley was next in line to the throne of England. We cannot know for sure if Mary's feelings for Darnley were reciprocated, but we do know that he was aware of the powerful position this would put him in. If he didn't, his scheming father, Mathew Stewart, the Earl of Lennox, certainly did. Many of Mary's Protestant nobles, including her half-brother James Stewart, the Earl of Moray, were strongly opposed to the marriage and openly turned against their queen, bringing the country close to civil war. However, Mary's loyal forces, now led by James Hepburn, the Earl of Bothwell, were greater in number, so Moray and his fellow rebels fled to England where Queen Elizabeth I shared their concerns.

It was not long before Mary became painfully aware that her husband was an immature, violent, drunken, embarrassing waste of space and not surprisingly her attitude towards him changed. Nevertheless, even if he was not formally to be crowned as a king, he was still the Queen's husband. Though there were undoubtedly nobles in Scotland who simply wanted what was right for the country, it does seem to be the case that too many were constantly going round looking for a convenient back to stab, and it is this latter group who now tried to use the vain and gullible Darnley to get at Mary. They knew he was furious that Mary had side-lined him as her closest advisor in favour of an Italian musician by the name of David Rizzio, who was appointed as her secretary, so they tried to persuade him that Mary was having an affair with Rizzio. Some would have us believe that Rizzio had indeed been having an affair; not with Mary, but with her husband Lord Darnley himself!

Either way, Darnley was insanely jealous and signed a pact with the rebels. One night in March 1566, Darnley, accompanied by a group of senior nobles, stormed into Mary's chambers at Holyrood Palace and brutally murdered Rizzio. The Queen was restrained by her husband as she helplessly listened to her favourite servant's dying screams. If you are starting to think this is all beginning to sound like some kind of badly written daytime television soap opera, I would have to agree. Even if you strip away the fictionalised elements we know to have been added over the years, you are left with a basic plot that is still pretty hard to believe. Mary's next actions, I would suggest, prove that she was not the weak indecisive figure that we are sometimes led to believe. Whatever her feelings were for Darnley, by now she knew that at that moment in time, he was the key to her survival. Somehow she talked him into betraying his fellow conspirators and together they escaped from Edinburgh. Mary Queen of Scots had to retain control, so she raised her loyal forces and, within days, returned to the city. In an attempt to create unity, she now chose to pardon the nobles (including her half-brother, the Earl of Moray) who were exiled in England, but she refused to pardon Rizzio's murderers. Though understandable, this may arguably have been a mistake, as it did little to calm the tension between the Queen and many of her nobles.

On 19 June 1566, Mary gave birth to a son, James, but was she now fully reconciled with Darnley, her husband and the boy's father? At the elaborate christening ceremony held in Stirling Castle, Lord Darnley was notable by his absence, and later that year, Mary's affections appeared to be turning more towards James Hepburn, the Earl of Bothwell. Compared to the weak and petulant Lord Darnley, Bothwell was a strong and powerful figure. Did Mary now feel the need to have a strong man at her side? Was she simply looking for a protector? The idea that Mary Queen of Scots might divorce Lord Darnley now became an open topic though it is unlikely that Mary would ever have gone down that route, as it would have brought into question the legitimacy of her son. As nobles became more and more concerned by the "Darnley problem", dark mutterings could be heard regarding an ultimate solution. In November 1566, Bothwell met with a group of nobles at Craigmillar Castle, where assassination was openly discussed.

Two months later, Mary went to Glasgow, where Lord Darnley had been confined to his sick bed in the home of his father, the Earl of Lennox. Although there is no record of his specific ailment, it has often been suggested that he had contracted syphilis; a suggestion that, to be fair, may have been put forward by his detractors. Mary brought him back to Edinburgh and they settled in at Kirk O' Field, a house close to the city wall and little more than a stone's throw from Holyrood Palace. We will never know for sure if it was pragmatism or genuine concern for Darnley's welfare, but Mary now gave every indication that they were indeed reconciled and spent much of her time nursing her husband back to health. On the evening of 9 February 1567, Mary left the house to attend the wedding of one of her ladies in waiting at Holyrood Palace and maybe told her husband: "Don't wait up." Or did she know that it would not have been wise to return and had no intention of doing so? At 2 a.m., the city was rocked by a massive explosion and the house at Kirk O' Field was reduced to a pile of rubble. The partially clothed bodies of Lord Darnley and his manservant were found outside in the yard, but there was not a mark on them. They had been strangled. Henry Stuart, Lord Darnley, husband of Mary Queen of Scots and father to the future King James VI, had been murdered. Many believed, then as now, that Mary was complicit, but it is perhaps worth mentioning that the vast quantity of explosives used to blow up the house were actually stored under the quarters that Mary occupied. Was she as much a target as Darnley? There was no shortage of suspects, as pretty much everyone hated Darnley, but Queen Elizabeth of England and Darnley's father, the Earl of Lennox, were pushing for an investigation into the prime suspect, the Earl of Bothwell. Mary had been in his company for most of that day and knew that Bothwell was in his own bed at Holyrood Palace when the explosion occurred. She appeared to be convinced that Bothwell could not have been involved (well, not directly at least), so accepted that he should be tried for the murder of her husband, as she almost certainly knew what the outcome would be. It was no more than a show trial, as no evidence was submitted, and the Earl of Bothwell was cleared.

I don't think we will ever fully understand the whys and wherefores of what happened next as Mary either chose or was forced to take a path that was to lead to her downfall. On the 24th of April, Mary Queen of Scots was abducted by the Earl of Bothwell and taken to Dunbar Castle, where some say she was raped and subsequently forced into marriage, while others suggest she was a willing participant. Either way, we do know that Bothwell obtained a remarkably quick divorce from his wife and he and Mary were married in a Protestant service held at Holyrood Palace on 15 May 1567. Three months after the death of her husband, Mary Queen of Scots had married the chief suspect in his murder. Is it any wonder that the people of Scotland were scandalised and turned angrily against their queen? A rebellion was inevitable and forces who now claimed to be fighting on behalf of the infant Prince James met Bothwell's smaller forces at Cranberry Hill, just outside Edinburgh. In the negotiations that followed, the Earl of Bothwell was allowed to depart and go into exile, while Mary was arrested and imprisoned at Lochleven Castle. Why was Bothwell allowed to escape and not put on trial? Why was Mary never put on trial in Scotland? The answer is quite simply that too many Scottish nobles had too many secrets that would inevitably come to light during any such trials. I should perhaps mention at this point that Lord Bothwell fled to Denmark, where he was arrested and imprisoned for not repaying a dowry relating to a Danish bride he had jilted some years previously. He spent five years chained up in solitary confinement and had gone completely insane by the time he died. We must assume that the jilted bride had her own issues, as she arranged for his body to be mummified and put on open display at her local church. It was well into the 1980s before his body was actually buried!

Mary was now forcibly persuaded to abdicate in favour of her infant son James, and a regent was appointed to rule during his minority. That regent was Mary's half-brother James Stuart, the Earl of Moray, who had been waiting in the background, trying to keep his hands clean. Mary was the "guest" of Sir William Douglas at Lochleven Castle, where escape was all but impossible, as it is located on a small island in the middle of the loch. However, she somehow persuaded two young members of the Douglas family, George and William, to help get her out of the castle and off the island. While George summoned the Queen's loyal friend, the Earl of Seton, to Lochleven, the sixteen-year-old William stole the castle keys and freed Mary. After locking all the doors behind them, he escorted the Queen to a small boat and they rowed across to meet up with Seton, who was waiting with a small band of loyalists. The occupants of the castle, who were now locked in, watched helplessly as, halfway across, William threw the keys into the loch. Two hundred years later, they would reappear on the end of a fisherman's hook. Shortly after this daring escape, Mary's small force was defeated by the Earl of Moray at Langside near Glasgow and Mary had to accept that she did not have enough support to successfully counter the rebellion. She now had to decide whether to give up and return to France or look for a new way forward. Her advisors pleaded with her to head for the safety of France, but instead she turned to her cousin and fellow monarch Elizabeth I of England in the belief that Elizabeth would help her raise an army to forcibly regain her kingdom.

Upon her arrival in England, she was met by the deputy governor of Carlisle and escorted to Carlisle Castle, where she was placed under armed guard. Elizabeth sent a courtier to look after Mary and there is no doubt that she was given her place as a monarch and treated with respect and dignity. A gilded cage it may have been, but a cage nonetheless. Through their correspondence, Elizabeth was able to convince Mary that she could only regain her position if she agreed to cooperate with an inquiry into the charge that she had been complicit in the death of her husband, Lord Darnley. Eventually, though doubtless reluctantly, Mary agreed. Shortly before the inquiry began, Mary was moved to Bolton Castle in Yorkshire, where again she was treated with dignity but was still a prisoner. The inquiry began in October 1568, with most of the evidence against Mary coming from Scotland. Even at that time it was pretty clear that some of the evidence, including copies of letters (known as the casket letters) between Mary and the Earl of Bothwell, had been falsified, or in modern-day terms, "cut and pasted". By the following January, Elizabeth declared that Mary had no case to answer and had committed no crime, but still she remained a prisoner. In fairness to Elizabeth I, we have to accept the dilemma she faced. Although they communicated warmly, the two queens never actually met, as Elizabeth was all too well aware that Catholics throughout the land focused on Mary as the rightful queen and she was therefore a direct threat to Elizabeth's own safety. Deep down, Elizabeth knew that Mary was her rightful heir and probably did have sympathy for her, but it could never be openly acknowledged, as frequent plots were uncovered to depose her in favour of Mary. Elizabeth chose to believe that Mary played no part in these plots, but she remained a prisoner.

Over the coming years, Mary was moved several times and it is probably fair to say the respect for her royal position diminished slightly with each move. In 1586, she received a letter from an English Catholic by the name of Anthony Babington telling her of a plot to assassinate Elizabeth and put Mary on the throne. By then, it is likely that Mary would had lost all hope of ever being released, so it is perhaps not surprising that she chose to reply giving her support and urged that France and Spain be encouraged to invade England in support of her cause. For Mary, there was a problem in that two of Elizabeth's most trusted advisors, Sir William Cecil and Sir Francis Walsingham, had intercepted and deciphered the coded messages. They had created the first great spy network and didn't just know about the plot, for the most part they had set it up. Mary was caught red-handed.

Sir William Cecil, along with other advisors, urged Elizabeth to have Mary tried for treason. The trial began on 14 October 1586 and, over many weeks, the damning evidence was laid before the court, though it has to be said that it was not exactly a fair trial, in that no evidence for the defence was allowed and the grounds for applying the charge of treason against an English monarch were somewhat shaky given that Mary was also a monarch from a different country. Despite Mary's protestations of innocence, she was found guilty, and the sentence of execution was passed. Elizabeth was genuinely reluctant to sign the execution warrant and constantly found reasons to put it off. However, it was signed, and immediate action was taken to carry out the execution before Elizabeth could change her mind. Mary Queen of Scots was beheaded at Fotheringhay Castle on 8 February 1587. She apparently showed remarkable bravery and deliberately chose to wear a bright crimson gown, as this was the colour of Catholic martyrdom and that is, almost certainly, how Mary saw herself. On hearing the news, Elizabeth flew into a violent rage and screamed that she had not given her consent to Mary's execution. She viciously turned on the ultra-loyal Sir William Cecil who, at that point, possibly feared for his own safety. Perhaps Elizabeth was even trying to convince herself, but she could not escape the fact that her signature was on the execution warrant.

The story of Mary Queen of Scots has come up in almost every touring trip I have ever done, and it is one that frequently divides opinion among my guests. We sometimes forget that the historic figures we discuss were real people with real lives and real emotions, so it may be that the very human story of Mary's troubled life makes it easier to relate to her. Whatever the reason, Mary Queen of Scots continues to fascinate. As we drive along, conversations inevitably bring forth differing views relating to her guilt or innocence though I often have to remind my guests that, in her own lifetime, Mary was the target of propaganda firmly aimed at moulding public opinion. We have to work through the fog of already dubious evidence that has been further influenced over the years by heavily fictionalised versions of her life. I urge my guests to read works produced by those who have taken the time to study the life and times of Scotland's most famous queen and tend to suggest *Mary Queen of Scots* by Antonia Fraser. She does show a certain bias in favour of Mary, so I should perhaps admit, even to myself, that it could be the reason why her book on this particular subject is still my personal favourite.

11

John Knox. The Reformation

When I first started touring with guests, I was actively involved with the local tourist board for Inverness, Loch Ness, and Nairn though sadly this type of locally based organisation is long gone, as government agencies now tend to be more centralised. During the quieter months, they would organise educational trips for people like me, and indeed anyone who worked in the tourism industry. We would all pile into a bus and go round the Highlands with Ian Michie, the main tour guide in the area at that time, on a microphone telling us all he knew. Ian was quite a character, who spent much of the time telling jokes and perhaps too little time providing any real content. He would always insist upon the old cliché of never getting involved in any discussion about religion or politics and I have to admit, at the time, that sounded quite sensible. Well, it did not take me long to disregard that particular piece of advice, as they are subjects you really cannot ignore.

I should perhaps mention that I was brought up as a rigid Presbyterian in the 1960s when Scotland was still a fairly rigid Presbyterian country. When I was very young, we lived in the small Highland village of Balnain in Glenurquhart, and every

Sunday we would travel to the nearest Free Church of Scotland for the morning service. For the following ninety minutes, we would listen to doleful prayers, mournful singing, and a lengthy sermon from a text that always seemed to come from the book of Revelations. We would only ever sing psalms, as hymns are not from scripture, and of course, any thought of accompanying organ or piano music was completely out of the question. Joyful it was not. Upon arriving back home, we were allowed to do one hundred percent of nothing till it was time to attend the evening service, when we would go through a repeat of the morning though perhaps a slightly shorter sermon depending upon the minister's mood that night. During the early 1960s, church attendance was still very strong throughout the country though most went to the slightly more progressive Church of Scotland, where they at least had musical accompaniment, and they did sing hymns. Unfortunately, the Presbyterian Church has a history of splits, with the biggest having occurred in 1843. This particular schism led to the formation of the Free Church that my family adhered to. The more rigid churches, such as ours, tend to be more common in the Highlands, but Presbyterianism in all its denominations was, and still is, the largest religion throughout Scotland.

The Reformation that swept through Europe in the 16th Century eventually came to the shores of Scotland, but of course, it was to be a particularly Scottish version that would be adopted and the figure we remember best from that period is the firebrand preacher John Knox. We know very little about his early life, but we do know he was born in Haddington, Edinburgh, around 1513 and attended university at either St Andrews or

Glasgow. Despite having been ordained as a Catholic priest, he does not appear to have had a parish at any point though there is evidence that he also studied law and subsequently became a tutor to the sons of wealthy nobles. Somewhere around 1545, he met the reformist preacher George Wishart, who was openly proclaiming the Protestant teachings of Martin Luther. Knox was converted to the Protestant faith and began to accompany Wishart as his bodyguard till March 1546, when Wishart was arrested and found guilty of heresy. Apparently, he was resigned to his fate and dismissed Knox on the basis that one martyr at a time was more than adequate. George Wishart was burned at the stake in the town of St Andrews.

Shortly after this gruesome event, a group of reformist Protestants took their brutal revenge by murdering Cardinal Beaton, Archbishop of St Andrews, and then occupying his seat at St Andrews Castle. The occupation turned into a siege that lasted for many months, during which time John Knox agreed to join them as their minister. The siege ended when the castle was destroyed by French ships under the orders of the regent, Mary de Guise – mother of Mary Queen of Scots – and Knox was taken prisoner. He would spend almost two years as a galley slave on a French ship before gaining his freedom with the help of Protestant supporters among the English aristocracy. Upon release, he settled in Berwick in the north of England, as his anti-Catholic, anti-French views were more readily accepted there than in his home country. When the young, Protestant Edward VI died in 1553, his fervently Catholic sister Mary Tudor (Bloody Mary) came to the throne, so England was no longer a safe place for someone like John

Knox. He travelled first to France then briefly ministered to an English-speaking congregation in Frankfurt before settling in Geneva, where he was heavily influenced by John Calvin. It is here that Knox developed his own ideas for a disciplined, democratic Presbyterian church. It was also during this period he wrote the pamphlet I previously mentioned entitled 'The First Blast of the Trumpet Against the Monstrous Regiment of Women' which basically suggests that the very idea of a female being in a position of power is an unscriptural abomination. It was, of course, aimed at Queen Mary of England though he would doubtless have also been thinking of the Scottish regent Mary de Guise and her daughter Mary Queen of Scots. He may have thought that he could safely return to England when, in 1559, the Protestant Elizabeth I ascended to the throne, but not surprisingly, Elizabeth was deeply affronted by his writing and refused to let him set foot on English soil. That same year, Knox returned to Scotland when he was called upon by the Lords of the Congregation to take the lead in reforming the Scottish church. The self-styled "Lords of the Congregation" were Protestant nobles who had a political as much as a religious agenda. They were determined to end French influence in Scotland and probably saw the Reformation as a means of achieving that goal. The religious power of John Knox was something they could use to their advantage, but it is doubtful if they realised just what they were about to unleash.

In May of that year, John Knox entered the pulpit at St John's Church in Perth and delivered a stalwart, soaring sermon condemning idolatry in the Catholic Church. He was a powerful orator; so powerful that a large section of the congregation was imbued with a violent passion and fury that was subsequently turned on anything, or anyone, that appeared to be too close to Rome. Their attack on nearby churches and monasteries quickly spread to other parts of Scotland. The Scottish Reformation was underway. Despite her antagonism to John Knox, Queen Elizabeth was a pragmatist who listened when he urged her to assist Scotland in ridding itself of French Catholic influence under the Scottish regent Mary de Guise. Elizabeth prepared to commit English troops, but the regent's timely death in 1560 brought about the end of French influence in a more peaceful way. Scotland could now go its own way.

The Scottish Presbyterian Reformation gained impetus following the death of Mary de Guise, as it gave Knox more freedom to pursue his aims. He was determined that the arrival of the young Catholic Mary Queen of Scots in 1561 would change nothing, as he felt the tide was irrevocably turning in his direction. He obviously felt secure enough to openly criticise Mary and never missed an opportunity to do so. Knox was appointed as the ordained minister at St Giles Kirk in Edinburgh and was one of five ministers who wrote *The First Book of Discipline* which effectively established the pattern of the new Scottish church and how it would operate without the hierarchy of the Church of Rome or the Anglican Church. Papal authority was abolished, Mass was forbidden, and a Confession of Faith (Formal Statement of Belief) was agreed by the Scottish Parliament – and approved by John Knox. There were nobles and, indeed, clergy who were not always comfortable with Knox's uncompromising views, but he was at the peak of his power and, without question, the driving force of the Scottish Reformation, so for the most part, he remained unchallenged.

Despite the misogynist tone of his writing in relation to women in positions of power, we know from private correspondence with females close to him that he could be tender, emotional, kind, and thoughtful. He certainly had a complex relationship with women, not least the middle-aged, married Mrs Elizabeth Bowes, who he ministered to during his time in Berwick. There was even talk of an affair between the two, though at the age of thirty-eight, he actually married her sixteen-year-old daughter, Marjory Bowes. Elizabeth's husband and the rest of the Bowes family did not approve and promptly turned their back on both mother and daughter, who then (both) went to live with Knox. He had three children with Marjory before her untimely death at the age of twenty-five. At the age of fifty, John Knox took another sixteen-year-old bride, Margaret Stewart, who descended from the royal Stewart line. Mrs Bowes, his former mother-in-law, was not at all happy about this new situation and promptly left his household. Even for the time, it was a marriage that raised eyebrows and created significant malicious gossip though it does actually appear to have been a happy union that produced three daughters. Several years into this marriage, he was taken ill (probably a stroke), and Margaret nursed him till his death in 1572, when he was fifty-seven years old. As with so many figures from history, we have to not just make allowances for the times they lived in but also attempt to read between the lines of how they were portrayed by their contemporaries, both friends and foes. John Knox was a powerful, passionate, charismatic preacher who could readily convince people of the logic, as he saw it, behind his argument. He was intransigent, intolerant, and doubtless extremely difficult to deal with, but he did more to change Scotland's culture, outlook, and image than any other figure in our history. Yes, others would follow who were even more fundamentalist in their approach than Knox ever was, but he is the one who laid the foundations.

As a Scotsman who had a rigid Presbyterian upbringing, I am all too well aware of the failings and negative aspects of that system, not least the teaching of unworthiness that gave Scotland the massive chip it has on its shoulder through to this day. I am equally aware of the bigotry and general intolerance engendered by the traditional Presbyterian ways that still feature in some areas of Scottish society.

By the time I reached my early teenage years, we had moved into the "big" town of Inverness, where we would attend the Free North Church. Compared to the small austere country church we were used to, it felt massive, and yes, for a staunch Presbyterian church, it was, and is, pretty impressive. Though sitting upstairs on the balcony pews was quite a novelty for us, the overall atmosphere was not that different, as the pungent churchy smells of damp and mothballs still lingered in the air while the equally familiar rustle of sweetie papers occasionally broke the silence of the gathered congregation. I would have been about fourteen years old when I sat through an evening service in that church and, probably for the first time in my young life, actually listened to what the minister was saying. His chosen text was Revelations, 19:20, and from this, he built his sermon around the "mark of the beast". I struggled at first but soon picked up on the false prophet element even though I was still not sure quite where he was going with it. As he slowly moved towards his conclusion, I began to realise and, sure enough, he finished with a fist thumping down on the pulpit before proclaiming: "This beast among us, this beast that must be destroyed. The Catholic Church." After more than fifty years, I can still feel the rage that went through me that night. I really wanted to say something to somebody there and then, but of course, I didn't. This was the Free Church of Scotland, where you did not question, you just listened and accepted – especially if you were only fourteen years old. When we got home, I was sitting in the kitchen with my mother, having our ritual after service tea and toast, when I decided that I had to say something and let out how horrified I was by the minister's conclusion. Her first reaction was one of amazement that I had actually been listening, but she then went on to suggest that I had misunderstood and taken it the wrong way. I responded with all the vigour of an indignant teenager: "But that is what he said, Mam." "Yes," she replied, "but you must always remember there are some very good Catholics." Of course I am biased, but my mother truly is one of the most kind and gentle people you could ever hope to meet, and she would never knowingly wish to hurt or offend anyone. However, I'm afraid her response that night merely compounded my feeling of anger. In subsequent conversations over the years, I discovered that she had first heard that phrase from her grandmother and used it that night, as she, quite honestly, did not know what else to say to me. There is no question that, even in my lifetime, attitudes have changed, but I have to suggest that passive bigotry remains as part of the legacy of our particular Scottish Reformation.

Despite this, we have to acknowledge the work and education ethic brought about by the Presbyterian Reformation and there is little doubt in my mind that we would not have enjoyed the enormous benefits of our equally specific Scottish Enlightenment of the 18th Century without it. So, yes, there has been a very positive side that helped establish Scotland's place in the world. A few of my touring guests have already heard of a book entitled *How the Scots Invented the Modern World,* but for those who have not, it is one I strongly recommend. The pompous title is perhaps less of an issue when you realise the author was not a Scotsman but was, in fact, the American historian Arthur Herman. He does not deal with the specifics of the Reformation, but he does brilliantly allude to the part it played in Scotland's rise from relative obscurity during the 1700s even if he might, at times, slightly overplay Scottish identity.

The four countries that make up the United Kingdom are all culturally different, though in reality, we have a great deal more in common than we sometimes might care to admit. Now, I cannot pretend to understand every aspect of what makes the people of Scotland who we are any more than I can for England, Wales, or Ireland, but I do know that religion played a massive part, so the distinctive Presbyterian Reformation inevitably enters into any conversation relating to Scottish history.

12

James VI

Most of my guests know at least something of the life of Mary Queen of Scots, but the same is not always true when we come to her son and heir, James VI of Scotland. In many ways, it is understandable that the tragic and dramatic life of Mary should overshadow that of her son, but we really need to look at what was achieved in his lifetime and the part he played in those achievements. A terrified Mary Queen of Scots, in real fear of her life, was forced to give up her infant son when imprisoned at Lochleven Castle. She never saw him again. When he was little more than a year old, he was crowned as James VI of Scotland in the Church of the Holy Rude beside Stirling Castle as attending nobles listened to a lengthy sermon from his mother's bitter enemy John Knox. At that age, the new king would have had been blissfully unaware of Knox's sermon, but it did set the tone for an indoctrination process designed to mould him into a devout Protestant who would be encouraged to despise his "wicked" Catholic mother.

Following the assassination of the first regent James Stewart, Earl of Moray, in 1570, James's grandfather, the Earl of Lennox, was appointed and, following his death, the position went to the Earl of Mar, whose wife, the Countess, had already been entrusted with the domestic duties of looking after the young king. The final regent was James Douglas, 4th Earl of Morton, who it would appear was an effective ruler with a genuine desire to protect the rights of the young James VI. There was, however, a cloud over Morton in that he was still suspected by many of having been one of the main conspirators in the death of James's father, Lord Darnley.

George Buchanan, who has been widely recognised as one of the 16th Century's finest scholars, was appointed as James's head tutor. His form of discipline bordered on brutality, but there is little doubt that he provided the young king with an outstanding education. Buchanan had briefly tutored Mary Queen of Scots and, despite having converted to the Protestant faith, was fiercely loyal to her right up to the point of Darnley's murder. Thereafter, he viciously turned on Mary, and we can be sure that he let his thoughts be known to her son. James VI was certainly well educated, but his upbringing at Stirling Castle must have been pretty miserable, so it is hardly surprising that he was excited by the arrival of his French cousin Esme Stuart in 1579. Esme was in his mid-thirties, but the thirteen-year-old James was immediately taken by the sophisticated French charms of his new friend. It also gave this lonely young boy a link to his father's family, as Esme Stuart and Lord Darnley had been first cousins. As their relationship grew, so did the power of Esme Stuart, who was now given the title of Duke of Lennox. He used his influence to persuade James that the regent, the Earl of Morton, should be arrested for the part he played in the death of his father, Lord Darnley. In 1581, Morton was tried, found guilty, and executed. The Earl of Morton may not have been the most popular man in Scotland, but many of the country's nobles were deeply alarmed by this turn of events. They looked upon the obvious intimacy between the King and Esme Stuart with increasing concern and even began to wonder if he was a Catholic spy sent to undo all the work that had gone into creating a rigidly Protestant monarch. They were further alarmed when, at the age of fifteen, James was determined to assume direct control. In August 1582, Presbyterian nobles decided to act. William Ruthven, Earl of Gowrie, abducted the King and held him at Ruthven Castle near Perth, where he was forced to sign an order banishing Esme Stuart from Scotland. Though frustrated, hurt, and angered, the young King James had no choice. Almost a year was to pass before he regained his freedom, and you will not be surprised to hear that his first act was to have the Earl of Gowrie executed for treason.

To a certain extent, the effort put in to creating a Protestant king had worked, but few could have realised just how independently minded James would become as an adult. His education had given him an understanding of theology that allowed him to match, if not better, many of his contemporaries and this certainly helped him in his desire to rein in the power of the Scottish clergy. He was also able to use his intellect against his senior nobles and carefully managed expectations by rewarding those who he felt would be most useful. From the outset, James made it abundantly clear that he still believed in the divine right of kings, but he was nevertheless an effective monarch though there were times when he could truthfully be described as a tyrant. This was particularly the case with his subjects in the Highlands and Islands who he looked upon as savages who should be exterminated and replaced with some of his more "civilised" English-speaking subjects. He had a very similar attitude towards the Irish and later did actually pursue a policy in Ireland whereby the native population in the Ulster region was supplanted with English speakers who were, of course, all Protestant. Through to this day, the people of Ireland are living with the consequences of that policy.

In passing, I often mention to my guests that many of the people "implanted" in Ulster came from Scotland and I suspect that was the case with a number of my own ancestors who would have originated in the Scottish Borders where, prior to the Union of the Crowns in 1603, they were part of a bandit culture. They, and others in that area, were referred to as Border Reivers, which basically means they were cattle thieves who frequently mounted cross-border raids on their southern neighbours. Numerous Scottish monarchs had turned a blind eye to these lawless tribes, as their activities actually provided an element of border control. However, when James VI of Scotland also became James I of England, they were no longer required, so in an attempt to "clean up" the border region, people living there (including the Johnstones) were made an offer they simply could not refuse. Knowing they had little choice, many of these Scottish Border Reivers headed for a new life in Ulster in the north of Ireland. This gave us the term "Ulster Scots" though many who later emigrated to America would refer to themselves as Scots Irish.

In October 1589, the twenty-three-year-old James married fifteen-year-old Anne of Denmark. By all accounts, it was a successful union that produced eight children though only three survived through to adulthood. After the birth of their children, James's attitude to Anne changed and they began to live more independent lives. Some have speculated that any marriage problems may have been a consequence of well-documented evidence that James preferred the company of handsome young men.

It has also been suggested that the King's preferences may have been, at least in part, behind a particularly curious incident involving the young Earl of Gowrie, whose father James had executed. It is a story I enjoy telling to my guests as we travel along, not least because it has never been resolved. The only full record comes from King James himself and goes into considerable detail, so the following is an abridged version. While staying at Falkland Palace in 1660, James and a small retinue of his loyal nobles were out hunting when they were approached by Alexander Ruthven, the twenty-year-old brother of John Ruthven, Earl of Gowrie. He urged the King to accompany him to Gowrie House in Perth, where he had apprehended a mysterious man he came across in a field trying to bury a pot of gold coins. He added that, even though he had locked the stranger in a room in his brother's house, he had told no one, as he felt it only right that the King should directly interrogate this stranger. Despite his apparent misgivings, James decided to go with Alexander and took with him a small group of his closest companions. When they arrived at Gowrie House, it appeared that the Earl was indeed unaware of the situation, as they arrived around lunchtime and no meal had been prepared. As they waited, young Alexander and the King left the others and discreetly went to a turret room in the house to interview the stranger. When the King's nobles realised that he had been gone for some time, they started to look for him, only to be told by their host, the Earl of Gowrie, that the King had already departed on his own. As they scrambled for their horses, a cry was heard from the turret room at the top of the house. It was the King shouting for help! They desperately tried to break down the locked doors and eventually reached the room where James was being held to discover their king had already been saved by his twelve-year-old page John Ramsay, who had found another entrance. Young Ramsay and the King had managed to inflict significant knife wounds on Alexander Ruthven before throwing him down the stairway, where he was found by the King's men and finished off. A servant of the Gowrie family who had apparently been in the room helping to guard the King had fled from the scene. As for the mysterious stranger that James had been brought to interrogate – he had "mysteriously" disappeared. When the Earl of Gowrie found the body of his brother, he gathered a group of household servants and charged up the stairs to confront the King's men. In the ensuing struggle, the Earl was knifed through the heart, with that fatal blow again being struck by the page boy Ramsay. An angry mob, more loyal to their own Earl of Gowrie than they were to the King, had by this time surrounded the Gowrie Town House, so James and his nobles had to seek the help of Sir David Murray of Tullibardine, who had been attending a wedding in a nearby house, to negotiate their way out before returning to Falkland Palace. The bodies of the Gowrie brothers were then taken to Edinburgh and put on trial for treason and were, of course, found guilty. Now you could be forgiven for thinking this ridiculous act simply compounds an already ludicrous situation until you realise that James owed a significant financial debt, possibly around £80,000, to the Earl of Gowrie. This came through a loan provided by the Earl's father during his time as Treasurer of Scotland; a loan that was accruing interest. If the Gowrie brothers were found guilty of treason, their land and possessions could be forfeit to the Crown and, of course, the debt would be gone, so it was win-win for James!

James VI seemed anxious at the time that his version of events should be fully accepted, to the extent that he instructed church ministers to proclaim this from their pulpits. Needless to say, few believed it then and few believe it now. Could it be that James VI had set this up so that he could rid himself of the debt and gain a lot of land into the bargain? Equally, it is worth remembering that it was the dead men's grandfather who held a knife to his mother, Mary Queen of Scots, as her loyal secretary Rizzio was being murdered. Their father was among those who imprisoned Mary at Lochleven Castle. Was James settling scores, or was the twenty-two-year-old Earl of Gowrie following family tradition by attempting to kidnap the King with a view to gaining power for his own family?

We can all come up with our own version of what the truth of the "Gowrie conspiracy" may have been because, to date, the truth has never been uncovered. A few years back, one of my guests formed a very definite opinion that it had been a setup by the King to rid himself of the debt he owed to the Gowrie family, but she must have studied the subject in more detail when she got home, as a few months later, she emailed to say she had changed her mind and now concluded that the Earl of Gowrie was guilty as charged. There is a little bit of Sherlock Holmes in all of us. Personally, I am inclined to think that it was an attempt, however inept, to kidnap the King, with the handsome young Alexander Ruthven being used as bait to lure a willing James. What happened thereafter we will never know, but it is quite likely that James would have sought to cover up the real reason why he first of all went so readily to the Gowrie House in Perth then alone to a room in that house with Alexander by creating a ridiculous story about a stranger with a pot of gold. Such a scandal would have caused him some damage in Scotland, but he had his eyes further afield to England, where he hoped to inherit the Crown, so could not risk any kind of scandal; he would do whatever he had to do to safeguard his reputation. After finding the corpses of the dead brothers guilty of treason, he took away all the Ruthven family land and divided it between himself and his favoured nobles. He then banished the very name of Ruthven, so even Ruthven Castle, near Perth, was renamed as Huntingtower Castle, as it still is today. Scone Abbey, another Ruthven property, was handed over to Sir David Murray. A thank you for his help in quelling the Perth mobs? The young page boy, John Ramsay, was also well looked after, as James gifted him both land and titles. Payment for his silence?

Queen Elizabeth I died in the early hours of 24 March 1603 and, three days later, James VI of Scotland received the news that he had been officially declared as the rightful heir to the English throne. He was now to replace the Queen, who had signed his own mother's death warrant and, of course, his desire to wear the English crown was the reason why, at the time, he did little or nothing to help her. Queen Elizabeth had never formally accepted James as her heir, but he did have an ally at the English Court and that was Elizabeth's very powerful advisor, Sir Robert Cecil. James VI of Scotland was also now James I of England and, basically, he could not leave Scotland fast enough. Within her lifetime, Elizabeth I had been recognised as a great monarch, but towards the end of her long reign, weariness set in and the glamour of her court faded, so among the people in general, hopes were high for a new dawn under James I, though not all of his English nobles shared that view since they knew James would try to curb their power, as he had done with his Scottish nobles. He also tried to browbeat the clergy in England with his knowledge of theology – again, as he had done in Scotland – but with limited success. Instead, he somehow managed to antagonise all sides, whether Puritan or Catholic. At all times, he clung to the principle of the divine right of kings and the following, in his own words, makes that abundantly clear: "Kings are justly called gods for they exercise a manner or resemblance of divine power upon earth.".

In 1604, James arranged a conference at Hampton Court with the aim of finding common ground between the Church of England and Puritans who felt that the English Church was still too close to the Church of Rome. James was very much in favour of a proposal by Puritans that a new, revised version of the Bible should be produced, though his Church of England Bishops were not so keen. However, with the King's backing, the project was definitely going to proceed, so groups of translators were appointed and set to work. This was a mammoth task that took seven years to complete, but it turned out to be a masterpiece of the English language for which James VI was happy to take the credit even if, as we are led to believe, he personally contributed very little. However, it is known that James was very unhappy that the Geneva Bible frequently used the word "tyrant" in relation to monarchs, yet this word does not appear anywhere in the King James Bible. A coincidence? We also know that James was fascinated by witchcraft and even wrote a book on the subject, so is it another coincidence that the revised version of the Bible should take a much tougher line than previous known scripture with a new verse in Exodus 22:18: "Thou shalt not suffer a witch to live." It is difficult to escape the conclusion that James did indeed influence certain parts. This interest in witchcraft combined with James's general paranoia was used by his contemporary William Shakespeare in the play *Macbeth*, which we can be pretty certain was written for the King.

The sense of paranoia related to a constant fear of assassination and it has to be said that James had every right to be concerned, as a number of attempts were made on his life. The closest was the Gunpowder Plot in 1605, when a group of Catholic dissenters stored a massive quantity of explosives under the Houses of Parliament with the intention of killing the King and Members of Parliament when they were due to attend on the 5th of November. There is a certain intrigue surrounding the uncovering of this plot, but it is worth remembering that Sir Robert Cecil, who had previously been the senior advisor and spymaster to Elizabeth I, was now serving

James I in the same capacity. Just before midnight on the 4th of November, Guy Fawkes was found guarding the explosives he and others had placed in the cellar beneath the Parliament buildings. Under torture, Fawkes gave up the names of his co-conspirators, including their leader Robert Catesby. They were tried and executed for treason. Their actions were to result in even greater repression for Catholics throughout England and the following year, Parliament declared that the 5th of November should be a day of remembrance and celebration throughout Britain. Ever since, on this day, we build bonfires, put a "Guy" on the top (an effigy of Guy Fawkes), and let off fireworks. As with many "quaint" traditional festivals celebrated today, its roots are in the suppression of one group by another.

Apart from a brief honeymoon period in 1603, when he took over the English Crown, I am not sure that the people of England ever really trusted James I, but for that matter, I am equally not so sure that he was particularly trusted as James VI of Scotland. Despite this, he should perhaps be remembered as a monarch who had more successes than failures and we should note that he was widely mourned when he died in 1625. Perhaps the most interesting comment came from Henry IV of France when he described James as "the wisest fool in Christendom".

James I would be followed by his son Charles I, but it is equally worth noting that his daughter Elizabeth was betrothed to Frederic V, Count Palatine of the Rhine. This strongly Protestant union with Germanic royalty would become very significant in future generations.

13

Charles I

Following the death of James I of England (VI of Scotland), his oldest surviving son Charles was crowned as king. Charles I, like his father, was utterly convinced of the divine right of kings though he appeared to lack the political instinct required to navigate his way through the authority of Parliament. His uncompromising response was to simply dismiss Parliament and rule by Royal Prerogative. As Charles would discover, a king who continually insists upon sticking his head in the sand ultimately risks having it removed.

He was only three years old when the Scottish and English Crowns were united under his father, so despite the fact that he was the last king born in Scotland, he did not really have any great knowledge of the country of his birth though he was very aware of his position as monarch of that separate kingdom. He was a weak and sickly child who appeared to lack confidence, but, cruel though this may sound, Charles was the younger brother, so it was not a great cause for concern. However, things were to change when his more charismatic older brother Prince Henry died of typhoid fever at the age of eighteen. It was already clear that the young Henry had intended to push the country towards a more radical Puritan form of Protestantism when he became king, but this was not to be. Charles, whose religious views were much closer to those of his parents, would now be hurriedly prepared as the new heir to the throne. Charles I was crowned in 1625 when he was twenty-five years old. He was much more inclined towards the High Anglican Church which was, at least in Scotland, seen as still being far too close to Roman Catholicism; a perception that was not helped by his marriage to the devout Catholic French princess, Henrietta Maria. Most of the tension between Charles and his English Parliament related to finance, as he frequently engaged in costly wars with France and Spain. When he chose to dismiss Parliament in 1629, he effectively cut off his source of tax revenue, so he decided to raise funds by other, dubious, means, such as enforced loans, imposition of custom duties, and the collection of "Ship Money" from counties with a coastline. He may well have stretched the law, but judges did support him and this method of raising funds proved to be remarkably successful over an eleven-year period. Unfortunately, he remained blind to the fact that it also succeeded in alienating even more of his subjects.

Like his father, he chose to impose his ideas directly on the church and, in conjunction with William Laud, the Archbishop of Canterbury, he came up with a new Common Book of Prayer that was intended to unify Christian worship throughout his three kingdoms. The King and Archbishop were well aware that this would not go down well in Scotland but proceeded on the basis of a long-held conviction that the power of the Presbyterian Church had to be curtailed. It was a serious error of judgement that proved just how little Charles knew about the land of his birth. The new prayer book, to be used at all services in Scotland, was introduced on Sunday 23 July 1637. Clergy in Scotland obeyed the order from the King and Archbishop even though they feared, and prepared for, potential conflict. It is said that the Bishop of Brechin conducted the service that day with two loaded pistols by his side. When the Dean of St Giles Cathedral in Edinburgh started to read from the book, he was first shouted down, then came under assault, with bibles being used as missiles. When the Bishop of Edinburgh entered the pulpit to try and calm the situation, it was not bibles that were thrown at him; now it was stools the congregation had been sitting on. The subsequent riot that broke out in the streets of the capital quickly spread throughout Scotland. At that point in time, England had been enjoying a period free of conflict, but soon it would be at war again; this time, the fighting would be within Charles's own kingdoms. In February 1638, a group of Scottish nobles gathered at Greyfriars Church in Edinburgh to sign a National Covenant promising to defend the Presbyterian Church of Scotland against any attempt to impose the Anglican liturgy. More importantly, this document was a direct challenge to Charles I and his belief in the divine right of kings. Most of Scotland's church ministers and nobility signed the covenant along with thousands of ordinary citizens. There would be no place for bishops in the Presbyterian Church other than as administrators with absolutely no authority over the governance of the church. Strangely, these Covenanters still insisted upon loyalty to the King though goodness knows how they were going to square that particular circle. They neither could nor would.

Both Charles and the Covenanters raised armies and, after

what might best be described as a series of manoeuvres by both sides, a meeting was called in Berwick to discuss a treaty that was duly signed on 19 June 1639. Both sides agreed to disband their armies. Given their comparative military weakness, the Covenanters conceded significantly more than they would have wished, so the situation was by no means resolved. Charles was fully aware of this and reconvened Parliament in order to raise funds for a new army. They were reluctant to do so, as many English nobles sympathised with the Scottish Covenanters, so again, Charles had to raise his own army. However, now that Parliament was sitting, it could begin to scrutinise the effects of the King's direct rule during the previous eleven years. Instead of funds, Charles was presented with the "Grand Remonstrance", which was basically a very long list of complaints relating to the way he had been governing the country.

The Covenanters in Scotland had regrouped and now engaged with Charles in the Second Bishops War. By late 1640, the Covenanting army had gained control in most of northern England, and Charles was forced into a humiliating defeat. An end to hostilities was agreed when both sides signed the Treaty of Ripon on the 14th of October, but in reality, still nothing had really been resolved. The following year, Charles entered the English Parliament with the intention of arresting five senior parliamentarians who were doing everything in their power to undermine his authority. Sensibly, they were not in attendance that day, but this act by the King was to lead, inexorably, to civil war. By 1643, it became clear to the English Parliament that they needed Scotland's help to defeat the King, so a contract known as the "Solemn League and Covenant" was drawn up. The Scots' primary objective was never to replace the King, but yes, he had to be defeated and then persuaded to establish Presbyterianism throughout all three kingdoms. The ultimate aim of the English Parliament may have been less clear at this point, but the emergence of the fervently Protestant Oliver Cromwell and his new, well trained, disciplined "Model Army", mostly consisting of Puritan soldiers, would have encouraged the Scots to feel they were pursuing the same agenda. The opposing sides came to be known as Cavaliers and Round Heads, with the latter given that name due to the Puritan-influenced idea of short haircuts, whereas Cavaliers had the more fashionable (for the time) long hair. The conflict raged off and on till Charles was finally defeated at Preston in 1648. What was left of the English Parliament (the Rump Parliament) concluded that there could be no meaningful peace as long as Charles was alive, so the decision was taken that he should be put on trial for treason. On 30 January 1649, Charles I was beheaded. That same day, Parliament passed an Act forbidding the proclamation of another monarch and, on the 7th of February, the office of king was formally abolished. The decision to commit regicide was made by a small number of people with very little popular support throughout England and even less in Scotland and Ireland, so it is perhaps not surprising that those responsible had little choice but to opt for a republican model with a figurehead supported by the military might of the Model Army. The English Parliament would now renege on the agreement with the Scots to impose Presbyterianism on all three kingdoms, so the stage was set for further conflict.

14

Charles II

Charles Stuart, the eldest son of Charles I, was nineteen years old when his father was beheaded in 1649, though for their own safety, he and his brother had been exiled in France some four years earlier. However, Charles knew it was his destiny to be recognised as Charles II and was never going to accept the "republic" set up by Oliver Cromwell. The Puritan religion now sweeping through England was extremely alarming to the predominantly Catholic people of Ireland, so that initially appeared to be the best route through which remaining royalists could fight back. Cromwell, too, was aware of this and launched an attack on Ireland to make sure it could not, and would not, happen. Whatever one's thoughts on Cromwell as a soldier, a politician, or as an effective leader, it is impossible to ignore the brutality of his assault on Ireland. His outright hatred of Irish Catholics fuelled an attitude that was used to justify atrocities we today would not hesitate to describe as war crimes. Around 40% of the country's population perished, either directly or indirectly, as a result of his actions, so we cannot be surprised that within Ireland the general attitude towards Cromwell, through to this day, is one of utter contempt.

In Scotland, Charles started negotiations with the Covenanters even though he had no enthusiasm for their Calvinist-led form of Christianity, but he was a Stuart and to many in Scotland he was Charles II, the rightful king. Conceding to the demands of his Scottish nobility was essential if he was to gain their active support, so Charles, however reluctantly, agreed to sign the League and Covenant. By doing so, he now accepted the Presbyterian Church as the true Church and, by implication, acknowledged that he could not rule by divine right. In January 1651, he was formally crowned as Charles II of Scotland. This was the last ever coronation to be performed at Scone and, indeed, the last ever performed in Scotland. Having dealt with any likely threat from Ireland, Cromwell now turned his military might on Scotland, where Charles Stuart posed a very real threat to the new regime. His superior forces defeated the Scottish royalist army at Dunbar in 1650, but the following year, Charles personally led an army into England, where he met with Cromwell's Model Army at Worcester. It ended in a resounding defeat for Charles, who was now forced back into exile. Scotland was occupied by Cromwell's army and, by force, became part of the new Commonwealth.

In 1653, Cromwell was appointed as Lord Protector of the Commonwealth of England, Scotland, Ireland, and Wales. At the same time, a new Parliament for all of Britain came into existence, with each of the nations having representation. In many ways, it was the forerunner of the United Kingdom. Scotland was no longer a separate, independent nation, but it did not suffer the same way as Ireland, and that is most likely because Cromwell looked upon the Scots as fellow Protestants.

Though there was a particularly vicious attack on the City of Dundee, Scotland did not suffer the consequences of the policy of land redistribution that took place in Ireland and subsequently condemned its people to many years of extreme poverty. Cromwell may have been suspicious of Presbyterian structures, but scripturally, the Scots were closely in line with his Puritan ideas. I am not sure why, in Scotland, we tend to look back on the Cromwell years with a certain degree of ambivalence, but it could well be as a result of the less bitter experience we suffered in comparison to Ireland, though it is probably more about forgetting than forgiving. Oliver Cromwell died in September 1658 and, despite the position not being hereditary, his son Richard was appointed as the Lord Protector. This act of nepotism proved to be a disaster, as Richard did not come close to his authoritarian father. He quickly lost control of the military, as they clearly had little or no respect for him as their leader, so it was only a matter of time before he was forced to resign. He lasted all of nine months.

The New Model Army, under the control of Oliver Cromwell, brought about the republican Commonwealth and now, under General Monck, it was the army that would pave the way for the restoration of monarchy. Charles returned as King of England in 1660, bishops were restored to Parliament, and the Anglican Church replaced the Puritanism of the Cromwell years. General Monck secured agreement that would allow for religious tolerance and negotiated an amnesty for those who had opposed Charles, though this did not prevent the body of Oliver Cromwell being exhumed and hung from the gallows. The crown and all royal regalia had been melted down following the execution of Charles I, so a new crown had to be made for the coronation of his son, Charles II, on 23 April 1661.

After eleven years of Puritan rule, nobility and commoners alike enthusiastically embraced the flamboyant court of Charles II, who very visibly enjoyed living life to the full. Nobody seemed to mind how many mistresses he had, and the royal family easily overcame the scandal of his brother, the Duke of York (later James II), marrying a commoner by the name of Anne Hyde after she fell pregnant. Even the current royal family might have struggled with that last part! The arts flourished under Charles II and served to bolster and enhance the powerful image of monarchy, so it is little wonder that he became known as the "Merry Monarch". This is not to say that issues of religious intolerance went away, as there were still a large number of Puritans who looked on disapprovingly, but Charles somehow managed to steer a way through by not overly upsetting any specific group. It may well be that he actually upset all sides at various times but not enough to make them want to revert to the strict regime of the Cromwell days. He married the Catholic Catherine of Braganza, daughter of King John IV of Portugal, in May 1662, but it does not seem to have been much more than a dynastic marriage that brought a massive dowry to Charles. The marriage did not produce any children, and in any case, Charles preferred to spend time with his mistresses, including the famous actress of her time, Nell Gwyn.

Charles II never forgot the time he had spent in Scotland

being browbeaten by fervent Presbyterians and now had little regard for the home of his ancestors. Although, like his father, he was acutely aware of his position as the monarch of the separate kingdom of Scotland, he left his Scottish Privy Council to run the country. However, he made it perfectly clear that it would be their duty to ensure the return of episcopacy. Their task was made easier, as Charles was sufficiently politically astute to avoid enforcing elements of Anglican (Church of England) liturgy that were deemed obnoxious to many Scots. Equally, Scottish nobles were very aware of which way the wind was blowing during the early period of the Restoration, so many moved away from the entrenched position they had taken when supporting the Solemn League and Covenant. Despite this supposed air of compromise, there was still a significant number who were determined to retain the more rigid ways of the Presbyterian Church and, more importantly, retain their opposition to bishops, so it was by no means an entirely peaceful process. Fervent Presbyterian Covenanters were ruthlessly hunted down and summarily executed by the loyalist Captain John Graham of Claverhouse, or "Bluidy Clavers", during what came to be known as the "Killing Times". It is worth reminding ourselves that in 17th Century Scotland, the primary difference between Presbyterians and Episcopalians related to who controlled the church rather than any serious conflict over liturgy. Presbyterian churches relied on the authority of their congregations, whereas authority in the Episcopalian Church lay with bishops who were ultimately appointed by the King; it was still about the power of monarchy. At varying times during this period, many clergymen, both Presbyterian and Episcopalian, chose to leave the country and quite a few headed for America. This included James Blair, who became the first president of William and Mary College in Williamsburg, Virginia. Scotland's losses were becoming America's gain.

In 1665, the bubonic plague hit the City of London and the following year came the devastation of the Great Fire of London. Also, at this time, a bright comet was seen in the sky. Taking these things together, the people believed it all to be a sign of God's wrath for the King's policy of increasing tolerance towards Catholics, so anti-Catholic sentiment rose dramatically. This was probably not a good time for anyone to convert to Catholicism, but the King's brother, James Stuart, the Duke of York, did just that and in 1673 entered a second marriage to the Catholic Mary of Modena. To make matters worse, Charles had no legitimate heirs, so the Duke of York would likely be the future king. The thought of a Catholic king was abhorrent to most people of England and Scotland.

Charles II had signed a treaty with Louis XIV in 1670 that would ally England and France against the Protestant Dutch. A secret clause in this agreement brought a payment to Charles, directly from Louis, of £200,000 a year in return for England re-adopting the Catholic faith, and Charles himself would convert "as soon as the welfare of his realm will permit". He was doubtless well aware that he was "playing with fire" even if he might have had no intention of honouring his commitment to the French king, but his position was not made any easier by a parliament that was determined to exclude his brother James as heir to the throne. Just as his father and grandfather had done before him, Charles simply dissolved Parliament each time they tried to bring forward any legislation on the succession. Charles II died in February 1685 at the age of fifty-five, having secretly converted to Catholicism on his deathbed.

15

James II & VII

Up until the very early 17th Century, England and Scotland were two separate kingdoms, each with a separate monarchical line. However, from 1603, both shared one monarch and that, I admit, can be a little confusing. Scotland had six previous kings by the name of James, so upon the death of Charles II, his brother became James VII of Scotland, whereas England had only one previous king by the name of James, so he became James II of England. Scots can be quite sensitive about such matters and do occasionally point out that our current queen is Elizabeth II in England only; in Scotland, she is really Elizabeth I. To a Scotsman, this is all fairly obvious, but it is not necessarily so with our guests who frequently come up with a request to "run that by me again?"

As the second son, it was never anticipated that James would become king, so, as with many royal second sons, he chose a military career. During his younger years, when the family were in exile, he could not, of course, serve in his own country, so he joined the French army, where he achieved the rank of lieutenant-general and by all accounts was admired for his courage, judgement, and loyalty to his men. At the time of the Restoration, James had just been appointed as the High Admiral of Spain, but given the new situation, it was no longer feasible for him to take up that appointment, so he returned to England with his brother Charles II, who instead gave James the position of Lord High Admiral of the English Navy. He took his duties seriously and again built a reputation as a military man of good sense whose word could be trusted. Following a successful campaign in 1664, Charles I bestowed American provinces on James that had been taken from Dutch settlers. His title at that time was the Duke of York – hence New York. Given his military reputation and general popularity among the public in England, surely James had the potential to be a great king?

In 1660, James married Anne Hyde and together they produced eight children, though only two, Mary and Anne, survived through to adulthood. Mary was married to her Protestant Dutch cousin Prince William of Orange and Anne was married to Prince George of Denmark. While both his daughters remained fervently Protestant, James did not. Around 1668, he converted to Catholicism and, as with many converts, he embraced his newfound religion with a zealous passion. In 1672, the English Parliament passed the Test Act prohibiting Catholics from any position of high office, resulting in all civil and military officials now having to sign an oath denouncing certain doctrine and practices within the Catholic Church, including transubstantiation, as superstitious and idolatrous. As a devout Catholic, James could take no such oath and subsequently resigned from his position as Lord High Admiral. He could no longer hide his conversion to Catholicism.

By the early 1670s, James was a widower and in 1673 entered

into a second marriage with the Catholic Mary of Modena, a fifteen-year-old Italian princess. By now it was becoming increasingly likely that Charles II would not have a legitimate heir and would therefore be succeeded by his brother James. Even though Charles was also moving towards the Catholic religion, he was alarmed by James's dramatic fall in popularity, so chose to manage the situation by sending him away for a while. After a short spell in Holland, he was appointed as the King's Lord High Commissioner in Scotland, during which time he was based at Holyrood Palace in Edinburgh. Although it would be wrong to say his Catholicism was not an issue in Scotland, there was perhaps a greater degree of tolerance and, after all, he was a Stuart and that would always be important in Scotland. The City of Edinburgh actually benefited from having a secondary royal court in residence.

In 1683, a plot to assassinate both Charles II and his brother James, Duke of York, was uncovered. It was known as the Rye House Plot (after the location where the deed was to take place) and involved a number of senior nobles, including the King's own illegitimate son James Scott, Duke of Monmouth. The plotters had hoped that the people would rise up against the King, who could then be replaced by the Protestant duke. In Scotland, the very powerful Earl of Argyll had agreed to mount a simultaneous invasion from the north. However, the populace was very reluctant to plunge the country into another civil war and feared a possible return to the Puritan-style regime of Oliver Cromwell. A return to Catholicism was absolutely unacceptable to the majority, but few, if any, were willing to contemplate a bloody revolution in order to achieve that result. When news got out regarding their potential assassination, both Charles and James actually gained huge popular support, which gave Charles the perfect opportunity to clamp down on his enemies, some of whom were executed. The Duke of Monmouth was forced to flee into exile and, given his newfound popularity, James, Duke of York, returned to England, where he took up his place on the Privy Council. The Rye House Plot had backfired spectacularly and only served to strengthen the position of both the King and his brother.

James, like his brother Charles, had many mistresses and, yes, he was a confirmed Catholic in a predominantly Protestant country. However, in 1685, when he became king, he was still a popular figure and generally seen as a man of his word, so there was no reason to doubt his promise to "defend and support the Church of England". As a result, he was able to overcome a further attempted rebellion by his brother's illegitimate son, the Duke of Monmouth, who was again supported by Archibald Campbell, the Earl of Argyll. Both were captured and executed. James II should and possibly could have been a good king, but unfortunately, England was still gripped by a fear of Catholic domination and this would always be hanging over him. Equally, it has to be said that he appeared to lose any sense of humility he may have had when he was the Duke of York and began to act more like a typical Stuart monarch who believed in his own divine right to rule. In 1687, James issued a Declaration of Indulgence that was intended as a statement of religious tolerance for all faiths but actually led to seven senior bishops being brought to trial for refusing to read it out from the pulpit. They saw it as little more than an attempt by James to re-establish the Catholic faith, and they were probably right, though it could also be argued that he was simply ahead of his time. The words "religion" and "tolerance" are frequently incompatible and sadly that is true to this day; in 1687, they were completely irreconcilable. Despite this, James, for the most part, remained popular among his subjects and even among his more dubious nobles there was no real appetite for further conflict. In any case, James's only living heirs were his two Protestant daughters, Mary and Anne, so in the end, it would work out, though that may have been more hope than expectation.

Following six pregnancies, James's wife Mary did not produce a living heir, so it is perhaps not surprising that suspicions were aroused when a healthy boy (another James) was born in June 1688. Some even suggested that the pregnancy had been contrived and a healthy male orphan had been hidden in a warming pan and smuggled into the Queen's bedchamber. This conspiracy theory was mostly put forward by those whose worst nightmare had materialised, and that may even have included his own daughters Mary and Anne. England now had a Catholic king with a Catholic male heir. It was one thing to have a temporary Catholic monarch who would, in due course, be replaced by his Protestant daughter, but this new situation would mean something more permanent. Within days of the birth, moves were underway to have James II replaced. The King's son-in-law, Prince William of Orange, was invited by senior Protestant nobles to come to England – along with an army. This was to be an invasion by invitation. Despite offers of help from Louis XIV of France, James was initially confident that his own army would be adequate to repel the invaders and, numerically, he was right, as his forces were indeed superior to William's. However, James appeared to lose his nerve and ultimately decided that he would not confront the invasion. This is perhaps not surprising given that he was now openly deserted by his own daughter Anne who chose to support her sister and brother-in-law, as did many Protestant army officers who defected and joined William's forces. Whatever his motivation, it could certainly be argued that James II, however reluctantly, did the right thing and avoided the inevitable bloodshed of another civil war. During an attempted escape, James was captured but later allowed to go to France where his cousin Louis XIV gave him a palace to live in and the necessary funding to live the life of a king in exile. Whilst we might assume that Mary would have wished no physical harm to her father, we can equally assume that the last thing she and her husband needed was a Catholic martyr. James was to spend the rest of his life in France, where an observer at the French court was arguably quite astute when he wrote the following, "Our good king James was a brave and honest man, but the silliest I have ever seen in my life."

When Parliament was convened in order to decide what should happen next, it became obvious that members were reluctant to depose James as their king, so instead they declared that he had effectively abdicated, leaving the throne vacant. By April 1689, the Scottish Parliament had also declared that James had forfeited his crown though their agreement had by no means been a foregone conclusion. Scottish nobles may well have been influenced by a somewhat clumsy and threatening letter James had sent, which certainly did not compare favourably with the more measured and polite representations from William and Mary. Agreement was reached that the "vacancy" was to be filled by James's daughter Mary, who would now rule jointly with her husband Prince William of Orange. The idea of joint rule by William and Mary was little more than a public relations exercise to give the new rule an element of legitimacy, as it was William who would reign as King William III, though being a pedantic Scot, I should mention that he was actually William II in Scotland. That same year, a Parliamentary Act was passed stating that no Roman Catholic would be permitted to ascend to the English throne, and no English monarch could marry a Catholic. Many of our guests are shocked to discover that such a policy remains in place through to this day though Prince Charles, the current Prince of Wales, has hinted that he would seek to correct this situation if and when he becomes king. Ultimately, of course, it will be a decision for Parliament. When you consider that the heir to the throne only changed from the firstborn male to simply the firstborn child (effectively, royal equal rights) as recently as 2011, you begin to realise how slowly things change within the British monarchy. My guess is that many within the "old guard" breathed a huge sigh of relief when William and Kate's first child was a boy!

Whatever terms the Scottish and English parliaments chose to use, the fact remained that James II was deposed, and the already precarious position of Catholics within the British Isles was further undermined, so it is hardly surprising that this decision gave birth to a cause. It was to be known as the Jacobite cause (*Jacobus* being the Latin for James) and the aim of these "followers of James" was quite simply to restore the Catholic Stuart dynasty to their rightful position. Many years would pass, and a great deal of blood would be spilt, before this cause would reach a conclusion. The course of history can, as we know, be changed by "events" and this frequently related to births, deaths, and marriages within ruling royal families. The death of Alexander III in 1286 was one such change, as was the case 400 years later following the birth of a son to James II of England, VII of Scotland, in 1688. From now on, the British Parliament would seek to do a little more in terms of forward planning.

16

William of Orange. Glorious Revolution

William III of England was born in The Hague in November 1650. His father was William II, Prince of Orange in the Netherlands, and his mother was Mary Stuart, sister of Charles II. In 1677, he married the daughter of Charles's brother James, Duke of York, who, of course, became James II when Charles died in 1685. That confusing little recap serves to remind us that William of Orange was both a nephew and son-in-law to James II and, yes, William and Mary were first cousins. William of Orange may have been a "foreigner", but he had Stuart blood in his veins and very close links to the throne of England, Scotland, Ireland, and Wales. However, it is also quite clear that his loyalty to his Dutch homeland was rarely, if ever, far from the forefront of his mind. The people of the Netherlands had turned to him when France invaded their country in 1672 and, as a fervent Protestant, he led the resistance. Thereafter, he pretty much made it his mission in life to oppose French expansionism in Europe. It is most likely in that context that he viewed his invasion of England in 1688, and I think it would be fair to add that he had become a kind of "poster boy" for the Protestant faith.

It was William who strongly pushed for the marriage to his cousin Mary, as the idea certainly did not appeal to either her father James, Duke of York, or her (and William's) uncle, Charles II. However, it was a union strongly supported by Protestant parliamentarians and Charles could ultimately see the diplomatic advantages, so reluctantly conceded that his niece and nephew should marry. At the time of their wedding, Mary was fifteen and William was twenty-six. He was 5ft 6in tall, not blessed with the most handsome features, and had very little by way of personality; as for charisma, he had definitely been at the end of that line. You will not be surprised to hear that Mary likewise was less than overjoyed, but ultimately, she had no choice if that was to be her father's decision. For Mary it was a matter of duty, but for William it was an opportunity to exert influence over his Catholic-supporting uncles. It is tempting to speculate that he may have always seen his marriage as part of a longer-term plan to take control of England and firmly establish a Protestant monarchy. Eleven years after their marriage, that is exactly what did happen, and Mary was to put her duty to her husband above any loyalty to her father.

The arrival of William and Mary was quickly dubbed the "Glorious Revolution" and given the fact that it was a bloodless coup, you can understand why the relieved people of England were happy to use the prefix of "glorious". Nevertheless, it was a revolution that brought about fundamental changes to the governance of the country and resulted in very significant changes to the Royal Prerogative, even if the issue of the Catholic Stuarts had certainly not gone away.

Only months later, James II launched a campaign, with

encouragement and support from Louis XIV, to recover his kingdom and, not surprisingly, the predominantly Catholic Ireland was once again the chosen gateway. At the time of the Glorious Revolution, Catholics were in a small minority in England and Wales, whilst in Scotland they probably accounted for less than 5% of the population. This was not the case in Ireland where, despite the policies of plantation under James I and further land confiscation under Cromwell, Catholics accounted for more than 75% of the total population. Yes, this was a struggle between opposing sides to determine who should be the rightful King of England, Scotland, Ireland, and Wales, but it was also part of a much wider war between France and a Dutch-led Protestant European alliance. To most continental Europeans, and certainly to William of Orange, it was very much about controlling French power. With so much at stake, William chose to take personal command and arrived in Ireland in June 1690 at the head of the largest army ever seen in Ireland. On the 12th of July, the deposed King James's French and Irish forces, numbering around 25,000, met William's army of around 36,000 at a ford on the River Boyne in County Meath. Within four hours of the first shot being fired, it was clear that William was the victor at the Battle of the Boyne. Three days later, James returned to France and would never again set foot on British or Irish soil. Shortly after, in Dublin, William of Orange was recognised as the King of Ireland. This marked the beginning of the "Protestant Ascendancy", a phrase that is really self-explanatory, and ever since, the 12th of July has been celebrated by Protestants in Ulster. The Orange Order that takes its name from William of Orange was formed many years later in 1795, following a sectarian conflict known as the Battle of the Diamond.

There are times when a driver/guide has to be careful what they say, and that was certainly true when I toured with two couples a few years back. Before meeting up with me, they had spent a week touring in the Republic of Ireland in the company of an Irish driver/guide. He had clearly done a great job, as they had an enthusiastic grasp of Irish history by the time I met them. One of the men had Irish ancestry and took on board every single anti-British sentiment expressed, or implied, during the time they had spent there; probably to a much greater extent than their Irish guide had ever intended. He had a hatred of "the British" which I suspect was actually there long before he had been to Ireland. Much to the amusement of his fellow travellers, he decided that I somehow represented Britain and seemed quite disappointed when, for the most part, I made no attempt to defend the British position in relation to Ireland's history, not least because many of the policies pursued were indefensible. However, I did inadvertently fall into his trap when I innocently mentioned that Ireland was the only part of the British Isles not to embrace the Reformation, so their comparative historical path was inevitably going to be different as a result. He immediately shouted at me, "So it's the fault of the Irish because they didn't succumb to your Reformation!" "No, No," I flustered, "I simply mentioned that as a point of information." The subsequent hilarity in the vehicle briefly had a nervous edge to it, and I made an immediate effort to change the subject. All told, it was a reminder of how sensitive the Irish issue can still be, even for those who are far removed from it and, equally, a reminder that diplomacy is an important quality when you are a driver/guide.

It is tempting to suggest that the Jacobite cause was all about the promotion of Catholicism, but that really was not the case. Despite the very small number of Catholics in Scotland, there was strong support for James II and that was primarily a matter of history. The Stuarts had ruled in England for sixty-five years, but in Scotland it was a dynasty that went back more than 300 years and subsequently engendered a much greater degree of loyalty. To many Scots, William of Orange had usurped the rightful king and that was certainly the belief of John Graham, 7th Laird of Claverhouse, and Viscount Dundee, who could not, and would not, accept the Scottish Parliament's decision to recognise William and Mary as their king and queen; you may recall that the military-minded Claverhouse was directly involved in the brutal suppression of Covenanters some ten years previously. He would now raise an army to fight for his king with or without the agreement of the Scottish Parliament. He knew that many Highland clans were loyal to James II, so that was to be his recruiting ground, and by July 1689, he had raised an army of approximately 2,500 men. Although most were Highlanders, they were joined by a few hundred troops who had come over from Ireland. "Bonnie Dundee", as Claverhouse came to be known, marched his army south and met a 5,000-strong government force at Killiecrankie, just north of Perth. Despite being outnumbered two to one, fearsome Highland tactics won the day and government troops were forced to flee, leaving some 2,000 casualties behind. Jacobite losses were around a quarter of this number, but among them was Bonnie

Dundee. Although losing their leader was a significant blow, the remaining Jacobite leaders were still determined to march south towards Perth, Edinburgh, and Glasgow. Unknown to them, a newly re-formed regiment of former Covenanters was waiting just a few miles down the road at Dunkeld. The men in this regiment were known as Cameronians, who took their name from the Cameron Guard formed by the fervent Covenanting leader Richard Cameron, so should not be confused with the Jacobite-supporting Camerons of Lochiel. The Cameronians had sworn to uphold the Presbyterian faith and had proved themselves to be willing to fight and die for that cause, so the Jacobite army had more than met its match. After many hours of fierce fighting, Jacobite forces scattered and returned to their homes, leaving much of Dunkeld in smouldering ruins. The first Jacobite rebellion was over.

Despite fairly widespread loyalty to the Stuarts, there had been no great appetite for rebellion in the more anglicised southern areas of Scotland where, of course, they were also determined to retain the Presbyterian Church and that would continue to be the case in the coming years. However, the situation would be quite different in the Highlands, where most clan chiefs were strongly attached to Episcopalianism and generally supportive of the Jacobite cause, though religion was not always their primary motivation. There were, of course, exceptions and it would equally be fair to say that many clan chiefs waited to see which way the wind was blowing before making any real commitment. The powerful Clan Campbell were loyal government supporters, and it was clear that they were willing to accept William and Mary, so it is not really surprising that John Campbell of Breadalbane, a trusted Privy Councillor, should now step forward with a plan that would bring his fellow clan chiefs to a peaceful settlement. Breadalbane arranged a meeting of prominent clan chiefs to agree terms for the signing of an oath of allegiance to King William that would remove any doubts about their loyalty. Any plan to head off a potential civil war was welcomed by William, his advisors, and the Scottish Government, so a substantial sum of "bribery" money was given to Breadalbane for distribution among clan chiefs in order to assist them in making the "right" decision. Clan chiefs reached an agreement whereby all would sign this oath on condition that the exiled King James II gave his permission. The wheels were set in motion and a deadline of 1 January 1692 was set for all signatures to be collected though an additional incentive was added by making it perfectly clear that the peoples of any clan chief who did not sign would suffer severe consequences. Knowing the retribution that could be wrought upon his loyal supporters, James reluctantly sent a letter from France giving permission for the chiefs to sign this oath of allegiance to his son-in-law William, but it was well into December by the time it reached Scotland and very close to the January 1st deadline. Despite the difficulties, most were able to make that deadline, with the notable exception of the Macdonald clan chief, MacIain of Glencoe. He had gone to nearby Fort William where the Fort Commander, Colonel John Hill, informed him that he had no authority to accept his oath and instead sent him to Inveraray, though he did provide him with a letter stating that MacIain had genuinely attempted to take the oath. It took him three days to reach Inveraray where he found that Sir John Campbell had taken time off to enjoy Hogmanay (New Years Eve). This caused a further three-day delay, but he did eventually sign the oath of allegiance, which was duly accepted by Sir John Campbell, who provided MacIain with another letter explaining the circumstances of the delay. A relieved MacIain returned to Glencoe and shortly after received a communication from Colonel John Hill stating that he and his clan's people were now under the jurisdiction and protection of government forces based at Fort William.

For some reason, and we really do not know why, John Dalrymple, the Secretary of State and Scotland's leading politician at the time, had a dislike of MacIain of Glencoe that bordered on hatred. There is little doubt that MacIain frequently operated on the "edge of the law", but he was hardly alone in that, so again we cannot be sure why he was singled out, but he was, and the consequences were to be horrendous for the people of Glencoe. From among the signed copies of the oath, Dalrymple selected MacIain's and decided that the full force of the law should be brought down upon the Macdonalds of Glencoe as punishment for "refusing" to sign within the deadline. No account was taken of the letters from either Colonel Hill or Sir John Campbell.

A regiment of soldiers under the command of Captain Robert Campbell of Glenlyon was sent into Glencoe in early February 1692, though apparently no orders had been given at that time. They were simply to set up camp. Robert Campbell was an older man, probably close to sixty, and an experienced soldier though he was known to be something of a gambler with a pretty significant drink problem. It has often been suggested, perhaps rather cynically, that he had all the qualities required of a good scapegoat, should one be needed. The Captain also had a family link to the Macdonalds of Glencoe in that his niece was married to one of MacIain's sons, so there are certainly reasons to question why he was chosen to lead on this particular occasion. Given his family links, it is not surprising that Captain Robert Campbell would have been invited to stay in the home of MacIain during his stay in the area and likewise many of his men were invited into Macdonald homes throughout the glen. Most who served in this government regiment were from the lowlands, but there were a significant number of the Captain's fellow Campbells who were familiar with the Highland culture of hospitality and very likely enjoyed being with their Macdonald hosts. Most saw nothing unusual in this situation, as the soldiers appeared to be on routine patrols with the primary purpose of tax collection. On the night of the 12th of February, as Captain Campbell was dining with MacIain, he received a despatch from a fellow officer, Major Duncanson, whose regiment was guarding the south end of the glen. The orders included the following lines,

"You are hereby ordered to fall upon the rebels, the McDonalds of Glencoe, and put all to the sword under seventy."

They also stated that if Captain Robert Campbell did not carry out this order, he would be dealt with as a traitor to his king. Around 5 a.m. on the 13th of February, Captain Campbell and his men followed their orders and turned on their hosts. As the reality of this horror quickly unfolded, thirty-eight members of the Macdonald clan were killed, including MacIain, who was murdered in his bed. His two sons were somehow able to escape into the surrounding mountains, along with many of the women and children. In the dead of winter, you do not survive very long in the Glencoe hills, so many more died from exposure; how many we do not know, but sadly they numbered significantly more than those who died by the sword. When the survivors eventually came down from the hills to bury their dead, they found that every home in the village had been set on fire. Brutality and tragedy were nothing new to Scottish Highlanders, but this event was something very different.

It is difficult to escape the conclusion that the Campbells were indeed scapegoats, as this act was nothing less than an attempt at state-sponsored genocide. Even today it is difficult for a soldier to disobey orders, so should we really expect that, in 1692, a relatively lowly army captain and his men would have done anything other than carry out the orders they were given, however distasteful? To some extent, they should perhaps be given the benefit of the doubt, as it is hard to believe that, out of approximately 1,000 people living in Glencoe at that time, only thirty-eight were killed as per the command. There is no question in my mind that they did not fully carry out their orders, certainly not to the extent they were expected to. It is also interesting to note that Major Duncanson did not arrive on the scene till after the deed had been done.

As news spread, polite society in the south, who might normally have had little sympathy for the "backward" Highlanders, were understandably horrified. Likewise, pamphleteers, who were the equivalent of today's media, seemed to be determined that the story should not be allowed to simply disappear. By contrast, Secretary of State Dalrymple tried to justify the action and, even at this stage, continued to issue orders stating that survivors should be pursued. He was ignored.

Under such pressure, an inquiry eventually had to be held, but, surprise, surprise, no evidence of wrongdoing was found. Still the issue would not go away, so in 1695, another inquiry was held. On this occasion, it was concluded that Dalrymple, as the Secretary of State for Scotland, had "misinterpreted" the wishes of the King. William had again been exonerated, but Dalrymple was forced to resign and withdraw from political life, albeit temporarily. The strongest condemnation was reserved for Captain Robert Campbell of Glenlyon and his fellow officers – despite the fact that they were actually following orders. It was suggested that they should be put on trial though no such trials ever took place and never could, as it would have risked the truth being flushed out; a truth that would inevitably have led to King William himself.

I must admit that during my early years as a driver/guide, I would happily tell my guests the dramatic story of the Massacre of Glencoe and how the treacherous Campbells turned on their hosts, the MacDonalds. Over the years, I have often quoted lines from a very dramatic ballad that was written as recently as the early 1960s.

"Oh cruel is the snow that sweeps Glencoe,
and covers the grave of Donald.
And cruel was the foe that raped Glencoe
and murdered the house of Macdonald.

They came from Fort William with murder in mind.
The Campbells had orders, King William had signed.
Put all to the sword, these words underlined.
And leave none alive called Macdonald."

To be honest, I still do recite some of these lines when I am in Glencoe with guests and occasionally play a CD of the whole song, as it is genuinely evocative. However, I then have to explain that the story handed down through the generations is not a truthful representation of what actually happened. Yes, there were clan feuds, yes, terrible things happened and, yes, there had been previous bad blood between the Campbells and the Macdonalds, but the cruel event that took place in Glencoe had nothing to do with any clan feud. Most of the government soldiers present in Glencoe on 13 February 1692 had no connection to either of these clans, they were simply British soldiers carrying out the orders of their political masters. To that extent, we are at times complicit in perpetuating a setup, and attempted cover-up, that has lasted down through the years.

William of Orange may well have been accepted as the reigning monarch, but there was always a gulf between the King and his English subjects though to some extent this was bridged by his wife Mary who, as a daughter of James II, was seen as more legitimate. He was undoubtedly more conscious of this following her death in 1694. There is a certain irony in the relative unpopularity of William and Mary when you consider that more royal power was ceded to Parliament during their reign than ever before. The Bill of Rights approved in

1689 restricted the Royal Prerogative in many areas, including parliamentary laws, the right to impose taxes, the right to interfere with parliamentary election, and much more. This is also the Bill that excluded any Catholic from the line of succession. William's frequent European wars were costly, so his constant need for parliamentary funds might help explain why he regularly acquiesced in these legislative reforms. This need to cover war debt also led to William's support for the establishment of the Bank of England which, I have to mention, was primarily founded by a Scotsman, William Paterson.

If William of Orange was simply unpopular in England, he was extremely unpopular in Scotland, and this was not only because he had been tainted by the events in Glencoe. By the end of the 17th Century, nobles and business leaders in Scotland realised that the agrarian economy they had always relied upon could never bring real wealth. They had to find a way of joining the trading nations of the world, so came up with a highly ambitious plan to set up a Scottish trading post at Darien in the Isthmus of Panama. No one can doubt that it was a brave venture that had the potential to bring great wealth to Scotland, but there has to be a question regarding how well thought through it had been, not to mention the chosen location of what was mostly poor-quality land that had, in any case, already been claimed by the Spanish. William III was King of England, Wales, Ireland, and Scotland, but in conjunction with the English Parliament, he did everything in his power to thwart Scottish ambitions, and this included banning any of his English or Dutch subjects from trading with the Scots. The Darien Scheme would have collapsed anyway, but when it did, you can imagine how the people of Scotland felt about their king. I should perhaps remove my earlier, slightly smug, comment about the Scotsman William Paterson's involvement in the creation of the Bank of England, as he was also the prime mover in the disastrous Darien Scheme. He had been remarkably successful when it came to persuading Scots to invest in the scheme, to the extent that the nation was virtually bankrupted by its failure and that would ultimately lead to the formation of the United Kingdom. A weakened Scotland ripe for takeover?

William III had no children, so his heir would be his late wife's sister Anne, the younger daughter of his deposed father-in-law James II. Given the potential problem that Anne might also leave no heir, the English Parliament passed the Act of Settlement in 1701 declaring that the next in line would be the fairly obscure Protestant granddaughter of James I, Sophia, Electress of Hanover, or her heirs. The Scottish Parliament was not consulted and later passed an Act effectively stating that they would make their own decision about the line of succession which, in reality, was a suggestion that they might opt for the restoration of a Catholic Stuart monarch. This was enough to concentrate the minds of English parliamentarians, as there was no way they were going to open up a "back door" route to the Jacobite cause. Scotland and England, however reluctantly, were moving inexorably towards union.

Near the end of winter, in 1702, William was out riding in the park beside Hampton Court when his horse stumbled on a mole hill and threw him to the ground. Partly because of his already poor health, he never recovered from the injuries he sustained. William III (William of Orange) died on 8 March 1702 at the age of fifty-one. From this point on, Jacobites would raise a toast to the "small gentleman in the black velvet coat".

17

Queen Anne (The Last Stuart Monarch)

By the time Anne Stuart replaced her brother-in-law as reigning monarch, the main rival to the throne, her own father James II, had died. However, the Jacobite cause would live on through his son, and Anne's half-brother, who in the eyes of many should have become James III. As a fervent Protestant and devoted supporter of the Anglican Church, Anne would do everything in her power to continue the exclusion of the exiled Catholic-supporting members of her family. Anne was thirty-seven when she became queen and only two years previously had suffered the terrible loss of her only surviving child, the eleven-year-old William, Duke of Gloucester. She had married Prince George of Denmark when she was eighteen years old and, by most accounts, it was a happy union though George would never be given any status beyond that of the Queen's Consort, which may have been wise given the following, somewhat cruel, comment from one of his contemporaries: "Unless he breathes harder, he might be taken for dead and buried by mistake." Throughout their marriage, Anne was pregnant on no fewer than eighteen occasions, so the loss of their only surviving son must have been absolutely devastating. It was still possible that she might yet produce an heir, but her health had suffered, so this was looking increasingly unlikely.

Queen Anne's reign coincided with the emergence of party politics, where the opposing sides were referred to by the derogatory names of "Tories" (papist outlaws) and "Whigs" (horse thieves), though the difference between them bears very little resemblance to present-day politics, as most still came from the land-owning classes, and all had extreme wealth. They felt they were the ruling class and, to be fair, it was a feeling shared across all sections of society at that time. The main areas of conflict related to matters of religion and the prosecution of wars, with the Tories being the more traditional and the Whigs, for the time, more radical. Anne would have found this quite distasteful and, despite her natural leaning towards Tory ideas, she did, to her credit, attempt to take a neutral line. John Churchill, the Duke of Marlborough, was a brilliant soldier and a prominent Whig but also someone Queen Anne trusted. When her long-time friend Sarah Jennings married the Duke and became the Duchess of Marlborough, that influence became even greater. Sarah was a domineering figure who, alongside her husband, undoubtedly steered Anne towards Whig policies. Marlborough commanded English forces during the complicated War of the Spanish Succession when he won his famous victory at the Battle of Blenheim. Having prevented French domination within Europe he was, during that period, at the peak of his power. A grateful Queen Anne, with the support of an equally grateful Parliament, set aside funds for the building of a great palace as a gift to the Duke.

The resulting Blenheim Palace, just outside Oxford, is truly magnificent. It is a fascinating place to visit and one that cannot be mentioned without noting another famous member of the Churchill family who was born there in 1874. That was, of course, Winston Churchill, so I would also recommend a short visit to nearby St Martin's Church in Bladon where you see the relatively modest location that remarkable man was laid to rest.

Queen Anne, as with many monarchs before her, and indeed many who followed after her, came to realise that close friendships are a luxury no reigning monarch can afford, as it inevitably leads to suspicion and mistrust among others close to, and within, the royal court. Even the Queen eventually began to realise that Sarah Churchill was being seen to have too much influence over her, so Sarah, and subsequently her husband John Churchill, Duke of Marlborough, were ultimately dismissed. For a time, Sarah Churchill's Tory-supporting cousin Abigail Marsham replaced her as the Queen's favourite though I suspect that Anne was aware that, to some extent, this friendship was also being used to manipulate her. The top of the tree, especially the very top, is a lonely place to be.

Anne had spent some time in Scotland during her mid-teenage years when her father, then the Duke of York, was serving as Scotland's Lord High Commissioner. By all accounts, she enjoyed this period living in Edinburgh's Holyrood Palace though she did describe the Scots as "strange". Whether or not this helped her to understand the differences between Scotland and England we cannot be sure, but now, as queen, it was something she and her government increasingly had to face up to. The idea of a full political union was first promoted by Anne's great-grandfather James I following the Union of the Crowns in 1603. Though he did not succeed, the idea never really went away and, despite a lack of enthusiasm under subsequent Stuart kings, it may have arisen at an earlier stage had the country not been otherwise preoccupied with civil war throughout much of the 17th Century. The already strained relationship between Scotland and England was close to breaking point by the turn of the 18th Century, as both Scottish and English parliaments passed ever more provocative legislation. When Scottish parliamentarians declared that they may choose a separate line of succession, and by implication a Stuart over a Hanoverian, England countered with the "Alien Act" which effectively banned cross-border trading. A full union was not a popular choice in either Scotland or England, and that had as much to do with prejudice and general animosity as anything else though clearly there were very real arguments both for and against. Whatever these may have been, each side had their own overriding reasons. For England, it was security, as they had to prevent any resurgence of French influence in Scotland by removing the need for a border. For Scotland, the primary incentive was their dire economy, so, all told, a Union of Parliaments and subsequent formation of the United Kingdom was all but inevitable.

Queen Anne appointed commissioners to come up with a suitable treaty and, on 1 May 1707, the Scottish Parliament was dissolved. Its powers were transferred to the new United Kingdom Parliament at Westminster. Scotland would be represented, or we should perhaps say under-represented, by forty-five Scottish Members of Parliament and sixteen Scottish members of the House of Lords. Whilst it could be suggested that Scottish negotiators did a poor job, particularly on trade and representation, they really had few options. However, they could point to successes when it came to the retention of Scots law, Scottish education, and the Scottish Presbyterian Church, so it was not all one way. A new Union Flag, based on a combination of the blue diagonal cross of St Andrew and the red cross of St George, came into existence though the Union Jack we are familiar with today dates from 1800, when Ireland joined the union and an additional red cross for St Patrick was incorporated. Strictly speaking, it should only be referred to as the Union "Jack" when it is being flown on a war ship at sea, but nowadays most people would consider that to be a minor, if not irrelevant, detail. However unpopular the union may have been in 1707, and indeed for many years after – particularly in Scotland – it did eventually bear fruit for mobile entrepreneurial Scots who proved to be extremely adept when it came to trading within the vast British Empire. By the end of the 18th Century, it had become one of the most successful unions ever, though the wealth it created would only benefit a small percentage of Scotland's population at that time.

Queen Anne suffered a severe stroke in August 1714 and died shortly afterwards. Despite the 1701 Act of Settlement declaring that the throne would now go to her Protestant Hanoverian relative, there were prominent Tories who had kept up correspondence with Anne's exiled half-brother James Stuart, but they were overtaken by events and she was quickly replaced by the Prince of Hanover who now became King George I. Anne had reigned for twelve years during a tumultuous period in the history of these islands, though for some reason, she tends to be one of our more forgotten monarchs. This becomes all the more surprising when you consider the formation of the United Kingdom through the Act of Union, and the rise of England as a military world power that came about during her reign. Queen Anne, in common with many monarchs, was no great intellectual, but she did take her duties seriously even if she was, at times, overly influenced by her Whig-supporting close friend Sarah Churchill and later by the Tory-supporting Abigail Masham, though ultimately, it was Anne who made the decisions. It could certainly be argued that history during this period was mostly recorded by misogynists who considered that the duty of any female monarch was primarily to give birth to a healthy future king and, tragically, for Anne, that did not happen.

I derive immense pleasure from the interest in our history shown by so many of my touring guests, but even after forty years, I can sometimes be surprised by the level of that interest. Quite recently, in the middle of a conversation about Queen Anne, I was hit with the comment: "Jim, you seem to be very sympathetic towards her considering that she was a Queen of England who showed very little consideration towards Scotland." Even as I was explaining that Queen Anne was a British rather than an English monarch, I could see how her strong advocacy of a political union between Scotland and England, in contrast to her Jacobite relatives, could leave the impression that England was her primary, if not singular, priority. Not for the first time, I could see where my guest was coming from even if I could not provide her with a fully satisfactory response. To my way of thinking, Queen Anne's attitude to Scotland was driven by politics rather than any particular disregard for her Scottish subjects, so this was an occasion where I and one of my well-informed guests agreed to disagree.

18
George I

Even though Queen Anne was never entirely comfortable with the prospect of a distant Hanoverian relative being her successor, she reluctantly had to accept that Sophia, Electress of Hanover, as a granddaughter of James I of England (VI of Scotland), was the nearest Protestant claimant available. Sophia's husband had been appointed as the 9th Elector of the Holy Roman Empire, but he died before officially taking up the position, so the title passed to his widow and then his son George. The Holy Roman Empire was to some extent a variant of the Imperial Roman Empire and basically a confederation of kingdoms that today would mostly, though not exclusively, be within Germany. The chosen electors would "elect" the Holy Roman Emperor, who would be appointed after approval by the Pope. The French philosopher Voltaire described it as "neither holy, nor Roman, nor an empire" which is basically true, but they must have got something right, as it lasted from the 9th to the 19th Century. It is tempting to make comparisons with the current European Union though I suspect most historians would baulk at such an oversimplification. For anyone wanting to learn more about the Holy Roman Empire, I can recommend a book by Peter H

Wilson with the straightforward title, *The Holy Roman Empire. A Thousand Years of Europe's History*, though I should perhaps add that it is not a short read! As successor to Queen Anne of England, becoming an elector brought much-needed status to Sophia of Hanover. However, it was not to be, as Sophia predeceased Anne by less than two months, so it would be her son George Ludwig, Elector of Hanover, who in October 1714 was crowned George I of England, Scotland, Wales, and Ireland. At the time, he was something like fiftieth in line to the English throne, but fortunately for him, the forty-nine in front were all Catholics. How difficult would it be to find the current fiftieth in line to the throne? Not very, as it happens. At the time of writing, it is a young lady by the name of Maud Windsor, who is the same age and goes to the same school as Prince George, who is third in line behind his grandfather, Prince Charles, and father, Prince William.

George I retained his title as Elector of Hanover, as indeed did George II and George III in later years, so given that he was fifty-four when he became King of England, we should not really be surprised that it was Hanover where his heart lay. He never spoke much English and that was certainly a problem, but his lack of popularity was also connected to the harsh way he had treated his wife, Sophia of Celle, following an affair she had with the Swedish Count Philip Christopher von Konigsmarck. He clearly believed that it was one thing for him to have extra marital affairs – and he had plenty – but his wife had to be dealt with severely for doing the same. In 1694, the Count mysteriously disappeared, and Sophia was imprisoned in Castle Ahlden in Celle, where she died in 1726.

This may well be the reason for a never to be forgiven rift with his son and heir (another George) who was given the title of Prince of Wales when his father came to the English throne. Strangely, feuds between Hanoverian kings and their heirs would become a feature of the dynasty.

Whigs in the English Parliament had pushed hard for a Hanoverian succession, so it is hardly surprising that George was always more willing to listen to Whig politicians and generally tended to freeze out Tories and their sympathisers, which again is not surprising given that many Tories were closet Jacobites. However, the Prince of Wales was more than willing to lend his support to Parliamentary Tories and they, in turn, were happy to exploit his bitterness towards his father. George I and his son, the future George II, were fortunate to be living during the period of Robert Walpole, one of England's great masters in the art of politics. He was persuasive, confident, and a real politician through and through, with an ability to bring people together even if it meant working with his political foes. Around 1720, he achieved what seemed impossible by arranging a truce between the King and the Prince of Wales, though admittedly, it did not last. George I relied on Walpole's talents throughout most of his reign and that was especially true during the "South Sea Bubble" financial crash, which also occurred in 1720. At this time, Walpole was appointed as the First Lord of the Treasury and effectively the first prime minister of the United Kingdom.

Whilst the Whig party, under Walpole, were determined to sustain the Protestant Hanoverian line, the Jacobite threat was ever present and there were still a number of Tories in

Parliament who would have welcomed a Stuart restoration. George I left domestic issues to Walpole and Parliament, thereby allowing him to concentrate on foreign policy though it has to be said that, to a great extent, it was aimed at the protection of his beloved homeland. However, he was very aware that the most serious Jacobite threat came from within Europe, and France in particular. There would be further rebellions in 1715 and 1719, but each was successfully put down. George I died in Hanover in 1726, so it would be his son George II who would face the largest, and final, Jacobite rebellion.

You will have noticed, and may have been quite relieved to see, that I did not go into any great detail on the subject of the Holy Roman Empire at the beginning of this chapter. To quote a euphemism often used by modern day politicians: "It's above my pay grade"! As previously mentioned, questions from guests during any touring trip are something I really enjoy but will readily admit that I do not always have an answer for. Tom Kolb is a friend from Alabama who I have toured with on a number of occasions, along with his wife and members of his family. I think it was during our last trip in the summer of 2018, on one of our longer journeys, when his wife, sister, daughter, and others in the vehicle were firing numerous, wide-ranging questions at me, and I confess I was struggling to keep up. Tom, who was sitting in the front passenger seat, had been uncharacteristically quiet for a few miles when he suddenly cut across everyone else with: "I have a question. What colour is the sky, Jim?" He returned my puzzled look with a broad grin and I quickly realised his "question" was really aimed at his fellow travellers. It took a few seconds for them to catch up, but it was not long before missiles were hurtling towards the front of the vehicle, aimed, I am glad to say, at Tom's head, not mine.

19

1715 and 1719 Jacobite Rebellions

The rising in 1715 is sometimes referred to as the first Jacobite rebellion, though I am really not sure why, as that ignores the very significant events of 1689, previously mentioned in the section relating to William of Orange. There was also an attempted rising in 1708 when the French navy planned to land around 5,000 soldiers close to Edinburgh; accompanied by James Francis Edward Stuart, son of the exiled King James II. Bad weather, and the superiority of the English navy, resulted in the plan having to be aborted, so he returned to France without having set foot on Scottish soil. James II died in 1701 and his son, James Francis, would now be the Stuart claimant to the throne. He came to be known as the "Old Pretender", which simply refers to his disputed claim to the throne of England, Scotland, Ireland, and Wales. In 1719, James, the Old Pretender, married Maria Sobieski, who was a granddaughter of King John III Sobieski of Poland, and the marriage produced two sons. The eldest and subsequent heir, Charles Edward Stuart, would come to be known as the Young Pretender and, later still, "Bonnie Prince Charlie". The younger son, Henry Benedict Stuart, who had a fairly colourful life, became a Cardinal in the Roman Catholic Church.

The 1715 Rebellion was a serious threat to the reign of George I and primarily, of course, a reaction to his actual arrival from Hanover. John Erskine, Earl of Mar, had been one of the main architects of the 1707 Act of Union and was an enthusiastic supporter of King George I, until, that is, he was snubbed by the new Hanoverian monarch and appeared to rapidly fall out of favour. The enraged earl immediately headed north and, in his home territory of Braemar, raised an army to fight for the Jacobite cause which, by any standards, is quite a turnaround, so it is not surprising that he was nicknamed "Bobbing John". Mar was, of course, on fertile ground and quickly gained support among clan chiefs in the Highlands. The rebellion got off to a remarkably good start as Jacobite forces quickly took control of Perth and Inverness, whilst a second group of Highlanders, combined with Jacobite supporters in the Borders, marched into England. Having secured the Highlands, the Earl of Mar marched his army into central Scotland where, on 13 November 1715 at Sheriffmuir near Stirling, he met up with government forces led by the union-supporting John Campbell, Duke of Argyll. Not for the first nor the last time, it was to be a battle between very different forces, with the government side consisting of trained soldiers who were up against inexperienced and untrained Jacobites. This should have been a Jacobite victory, as they numbered around 6,000 compared to government forces of approximately 3,000, but leadership was a problem, as the Earl of Mar was no general. After fierce fighting, resulting in close to a thousand casualties, the Earl failed to push forward an attack that would probably have broken through government lines, so the battle ended with neither side being able to claim victory. Since they failed to break through and take central Scotland, the 1715 Rebellion was all but over. Many poems and songs were written about this inconclusive battle, but I cannot help thinking the following, attributed to a contemporary minister, Rev Murdoch McLennan, is the simplest and the most descriptive:

"There's some say that we wan
Some say that they wan
Some say that nane wan at a' man
But o' ae thing I'm sure
That at Sheriff Muir
A battle was there that I saw, man
And we ran, and they ran
And they ran, and we ran
And we ran and they ran awa' man."

The other Jacobite army, having marched into England, engaged in battle with government forces at the northern English town of Preston. After two days of fighting, the Jacobites laid down their arms and surrendered. Shortly after, George I brought in 6,000 Dutch soldiers to help put down what was left of the rebellion in Scotland. By December, when James, the Old Pretender, arrived in Peterhead harbour, it was too late, so on 4 February 1716, he sailed back to France accompanied by the Earl of Mar. Neither man would ever return to Scotland.

When you consider the size of the Jacobite army at the Battle of Sheriffmuir, it really is surprising that the 1715 Rebellion should have failed. Yes, the inexperience of their commander, the Earl of Mar, was a pretty decisive factor, and yes, there was a distinctive lack of coordination, but it can equally be said that the Duke of Argyll, who was commanding government forces, did not exactly cover himself in glory. On the government side, he had to shoulder the blame for the inconclusive events at Sheriffmuir, resulting in his dismissal and subsequent, though temporary, fall from grace. The rising of 1715 was probably the Jacobites' best opportunity, but much to the relief of the British Parliament, it failed. However, they knew it could happen again, so chose to act by ensuring a strong military presence in Scotland that would act as a deterrent and also allow for a close eye to be kept on Jacobite-supporting Highland clans.

The respected English general George Wade was tasked with building and upgrading a line of forts and barracks across northern Scotland, including Ruthven Barracks at Newtonmore, Fort George at Inverness, Fort Augustus on the shore of Loch Ness, and Fort William at the east end of the Great Glen. Roads and bridges had to be created to allow for rapid troop movement in order to facilitate what would, in effect, be a military occupation of the Highlands. By the time Wade stepped down in favour of his successor Major Caulfield, the Highlands had around 300 miles of usable roads, with many crossing rivers over "Wade Bridges" that, in some areas, are in use to this day. Another of the little rhymes my contemporaries and I remember from our school days goes as follows:

"If you'd seen these roads before they were made,
You'd raise up your hands and bless General Wade."

Alongside these measures came the "Disarming Act", aimed at taking weapons out of the hands of Jacobite-supporting Highlanders, though in reality, very few swords or guns were given up. Another, perhaps more astute, suggestion from Wade related to the formation of a regiment that was be recruited from loyal Highland clans so that they could "police" the Highlands. Given the vast number of capable young Highland warriors available, there was no shortage of recruits, so a new Highland regiment was born. Despite their origins, this famous regiment, with their distinctive Black Watch tartan kilts, would be loyal to the British Government.

There was a further minor rebellion in 1719 though this time there was no French involvement, as the death of Louis XIV had brought about a change in their foreign policy that actually led to an alliance with England. The change was such that the Old Pretender became something of a diplomatic embarrassment for the French, so he eventually had to leave for Italy, where the Pope provided him with a palace in Rome. This became the new Jacobite headquarters. The 1719 Rebellion involved an Italian cardinal by the name of Giulio Alberoni, an Irish Jacobite by the name of James Butler (Duke of Ormonde), and the Catholic King Philip V of Spain. A sizeable, well-armed Spanish fleet set sail with the intention of landing troops on the West of England, but they were defeated by a storm long before they reached the English coast and had to abort the mission. Not for the first time, people would talk about the "Protestant Winds", as it did seem that Catholic Jacobite plans were regularly thwarted by foul weather conditions. Meanwhile, two ships heading for Scotland survived the storm and sailed into

Loch Duich on the north-west of Scotland, where they were to rendezvous with Scottish Jacobite leaders at Eilean Donan Castle. Cameron of Lochiel and Mackenzie of Seaforth brought a number of their clansmen to fight alongside the Marquis of Tullibardine and his brother Lord George Murray, who was to command the gathered forces.

The notorious Rob Roy Macgregor also appeared with around eighty of his men, though true to form, he played little part in the actual fight. I should briefly mention the 1995 film *Rob Roy* starring Liam Neeson, which was filmed in Scotland at the same time as *Braveheart*, so, as you can imagine, it was somewhat overshadowed. I feel slightly bad (I did say slightly) at having to mention something of the real Rob Roy who, unfortunately, bore very little resemblance to the "Scottish Robin Hood" character we have come to know, though to be fair, it was Scotland's own Sir Walter Scott who portrayed him in this way. The real Rob Roy was a violent conman whose main "business" was protection rackets though it has to be said that he was also very handy with a pen and, during his own lifetime, had laid the groundwork for Sir Walter. However, anyone who believes in reincarnation should probably look towards Chicago in the 1920s and 30s.

On the 10th of May, Royal Navy ships entered Loch Duich, stormed Eilean Donan, and took forty-five Spanish prisoners before using their store of gunpowder to destroy the castle. The nearby Jacobite forces of around 1,000 men got word that a government army from Inverness was now marching towards them with an equal-sized army, so they decided to make a stand at Glenshiel, a few miles east of Eilean Donan. The battle started in the early evening and raged for about three hours, but the following day, a decision was taken that the Highlanders would disperse, and the remaining Spanish forces would surrender, as they at least would be treated as prisoners of war and would eventually be returned to their homeland. The short-lived 1719 Rebellion was over. Today, a memorial stone marks the location, though perhaps more fittingly, a nearby mountain has been known as Sgurr nan Spainteach ever since, which translates as "Peak of the Spaniards". After 1719, the Jacobite threat did appear to be receding, so by 1740, the government felt reasonably secure and slowly began to scale back operations in the Highlands.

20

George II

George Augustus spent the first thirty years of his life in Hanover before his father took over the British throne when, as his heir, the younger George became the Prince of Wales. At the age of forty-four, after the death of his father, he became George II and was crowned at Westminster Abbey in October 1727. He had been married to Caroline, Daughter of the Margrave of Brandenburg, since 1705 and together they had nine children, of which seven survived. During his time as Prince of Wales, George was often the focus of opposition to his father due to their fractious relationship which often bordered on outright hatred for each other. Given this history, you might have expected the reign of George II to be very different from that of his father and to some extent that was the case though he was fortunate to have the more diplomatically aware Queen Caroline at his side. When he attempted to dismiss his very capable prime minister, purely on the basis that Walpole had served his father, it was Caroline who persuaded him that, among the alternatives, Robert Walpole was still the most suitable option. His hesitancy soon disappeared, as, like his father, he began to rely on Walpole and, in 1735, presented him with

10 Downing Street – the famous home of every British prime minister since.

George II may have absorbed slightly more English culture than his father and, with the help of Queen Caroline, he had cultivated a number of friendships among the British elite. However, strong loyalty to his Hanoverian homeland was something that he did share with George I and this would continue to foster doubts, particularly in England, regarding ultimate loyalties within the early years of the Hanoverian dynasty. Given that he was still the Elector of Hanover, it was, to be fair, always going to be a difficult balance. This general suspicion was for some confirmed when George insisted upon British involvement in the Austrian War of Succession following the death, in 1740, of Charles VI, who was the Holy Roman Emperor and head of the Austrian Habsburgs. George II personally commanded the combined forces of Britain, Austria, and Hanover against the French at the Battle of Dettingen in 1743 and was actually the last British monarch to personally lead an army into battle.

Prince Frederick was George II's son and heir, but sadly the disastrous father-son relationship was to mirror that which George II had with his father. History was to be repeated, as Frederick, Prince of Wales, like his father before him, became the focus of rival opposition to the King. Prince Frederick was born in Hanover in 1709 but did not travel to England with his family when his grandfather, George I, ascended to the British throne. Instead, he remained in Hanover for the next fourteen years, where he was brought up by a great uncle. In some ways, you can understand the need for the family to retain a physical presence of an heir in Hanover, the country where they were still the official rulers, but it would appear that there was little or no contact between the young prince and his parents throughout this period. We might never understand why, but it may go some way to explaining the cold relations between Frederick and both his parents. When Frederick finally arrived in England in 1728, he was twenty-one years old and, by all accounts, he did try to foster some sort of relationship with his parents and siblings. With the exception of his young brother William Augustus, Duke of Cumberland, he had little success, as his parents and sisters continued to treat him with what could only really be described as contempt.

In 1736, George II arranged for the now twenty-nine-year-old Frederick, Prince of Wales, to be married to the sixteen-year-old Princess Augusta of Saxe-Gotha. Strangely, no reception of any kind had been arranged to welcome this shy young princess who spoke no English, so for the first couple of days, she was left to make her own way. Frederick was furious and stepped in himself to welcome his bride to be. Fortunately, they did quickly form a good relationship, and following the marriage, Frederick finally had a close ally. Sadly, the marriage did nothing to change relations with his parents, as they appeared to treat the new Princess of Wales with similar contempt. The princess very quickly fell pregnant and, perhaps by way of a fight back, Frederick was determined that neither his father nor mother would be there at the birth, so when Augusta was actually in labour, he had her bundled into a carriage, taking them away from Hampton Court to St James's Palace. An already bad situation simply got worse, as the King and Queen now banished the Prince and Princess of Wales from the royal palaces and arranged for them to be moved to Kew Palace. The King then made it clear that anyone who chose to visit the Prince and Princess of Wales would no longer be welcome at the royal court, and Queen Caroline made it very clear that she did not wish to see either of them ever again. Frederick did attempt to publicly apologise for his actions in the hope of improving their situation but to no avail. They would remain at Kew Palace, and it is here they raised their nine children during what appears to have been a happy marriage.

Queen Caroline got her wish, as she died only a few months later when, even on her deathbed, it was made clear that she did not want to see her son Frederick. We should perhaps not be surprised, as this is the mother who reportedly said of her son, "My dear firstborn is the greatest ass, and the greatest liar, and the greatest canaille, and the greatest beast in the whole world, and I most heartily wish he was out of it." Sadly, Frederick, the Prince of Wales, was indeed "out of it" when he died in 1751 at the age of forty-four as a result of a tumour on his lung. No member of the immediate royal family attended the funeral, and his unforgiving father was reported as having said that he was glad to be rid of him.

A difficult relationship between a monarch and their heir is by no means unusual, as it occurred both before and after the period of George II and his son Frederick. However, the bitterness here reached an unusual, almost sinister level that is very hard to understand. George II and Queen Caroline appear to have been loving parents to their other children, who all in turn, with the possible exception of Prince George Augustus,

Duke of Cumberland, seemed to share their parents' animosity to Frederick. Does that suggest that the fault lay with Frederick? Maybe, but it equally has to be said that Frederick, Prince of Wales, was a very loving parent to his own children and contemporary reports suggest he was popular among friends, with no indication of any serious character flaws. It has been suggested that the answer could lie in some unknown event that may have taken place in Hanover during his younger days, but the truth is that we do not know, so for now, it remains a mystery. It is not difficult to imagine what modern-day media would do with such a dramatic story within the royal family and the "spin" that might be put on it by each side, so when we look at this story, we should again remember the value of propaganda both then and now. We can only speculate about the kind of king Frederick might have been had he lived though we certainly do not have to speculate when it comes to his oldest son, and heir, who would become George III.

When George II died in 1760, he had been Britain's reigning monarch for thirty-three years. Though Britain was still at war with France at the time of his death, it was clear that French domination in Europe was waning and Britain was continuing to emerge as the main world power. On a domestic front, "war" within the royal family was obviously a distraction, but politically, the ever-present Jacobite issue throughout the reign of George II had been of an altogether different nature.

21

1745 Jacobite Rebellion

The arrival of an Irish priest on the South Uist Island of Eriskay was nothing unusual, as Catholics living in the Western Isles often relied on visiting Irish clergy, especially now that Scotland had become a predominantly Protestant country. Had any local spoken to this tall, handsome young man they would certainly have discovered his Catholic credentials but would have been shocked to discover that he did not speak the Celtic Gaelic language, nor did he have anything resembling an Irish accent. This obviously cultured visitor, with the undeniable bearing of a gentleman, mostly spoke in French though he was also fluent in Italian, Spanish, and English. He and his seven companions were quickly ushered from the harbour to the home of Angus Macdonald, a relative of the local clan chief, where they dined and slept on the night of 23 July 1745. The following morning, they returned to the ship that had brought them to the island, where they were met by the chief himself, Macdonald of Boisdale, who immediately told the young visitor to "go home". The reply was swift, "I have come home, sir, and I will not return to that place from whence I came for I am persuaded my faithful Highlanders will stand by me." Only Boisdale and his tacksman (senior tenant), Angus Macdonald, knew this was no priest but was in fact Prince Charles Edward Stuart, son of their rightful king and grandson of the deposed King James II of England, VII of Scotland.

During the Austrian War of Succession, Prince Charles Edward Stuart, with the blessing of his father James Francis (the Old Pretender), left Italy for France so he could join a large French fleet that would launch an attack on England. The fleet was defeated by storms before they reached England's coast, so yet again, Jacobite plans were thwarted by circumstances beyond their control. Despite this setback, Charles remained in France, as Louis XV had assured him he would provide the funds and military support for a future campaign when the time was right. As months went by, the young, adventurous prince became increasingly frustrated and, with growing impatience, chose to take matters into his own hands. By a combination of borrowing where he could and selling of some of his family's priceless jewellery, he somehow managed to acquire the services of two fully crewed ships, *La Doutelle* and the *Elizabeth*. On 5 July 1745, the two ships set sail for Scotland, with Charles, a small retinue of his personal staff, and seven of his main advisors on board the *La Doutelle*. Supplies of arms and possibly gold, to finance the rebellion, were carried on the *Elizabeth*, but disaster soon struck when it came under attack from a British warship. The captain had no choice but to return his ship to harbour. Now, when Charles became aware of this major setback, you really would think that he would have taken the safe, not to mention sensible, option of giving up and returning to France, but no, his determination was undiminished. Yes, it was foolhardy, and yes, this showed a degree of arrogance, but his personal courage, and the courage of his convictions, surely cannot be doubted. Should we really pay any attention to the frequent portrayal over the years of Prince Charles Edward Stuart as an effete, weak character? No, we should not, as courage is the one thing he clearly did not lack. His boundless optimism was grounded in stories he had heard all his life about the bravery of loyal Highland clans, who he was now convinced would rush to join his cause and provide him with an instant army as soon as he arrived in Scotland.

Macdonald of Boisdale did not just tell the prince to go home, he also let him know that the powerful clan chiefs Macdonald of Sleat and Macleod of Dunvegan would not join any rebellion without an absolute guarantee of direct French support. Even this did nothing to deter Charles, who was making it very clear that no was not an answer he was going to accept. On the 25th of July, he left Eriskay for the Scottish mainland. When his ship *La Doutelle* anchored in Loch nan Uamh in the Moidart area, on the west coast, he continued to send out messages to clan leaders asking that they meet at Glenfinnan around midday on the 19th of August, with all the men they could muster. The area was carefully chosen, as it was within reasonable reach of many supportive clans but sufficiently remote to help in keeping the enterprise as secret as possible though the British Government were, in truth, well aware that Prince Charles Edward Stuart had landed in Scotland, even if they could not successfully track his movements. They were also aware that his father had given him the official position of regent to act on his behalf and would, from now on, frequently refer to him as the "Young Pretender".

On the morning of the 19th of August, Prince Charles and his companions, who would come to be known as the "Seven Men of Moidart", rowed a small boat up Loch Shiel to Glenfinnan where they were met by the embarrassingly small number of fifty Macdonalds from the local area. Shortly after, they were joined by a further group of 150 Macdonalds, but it would not be much of a rebellion with only 200 men. As the afternoon wore on, many of those present began to think this whole venture might be all over before it had even begun, but later in the afternoon, spirits lifted as the skirl of bagpipes could be heard in the distance. As men scrambled up the nearest hills for a vantage point, the message came back to the prince that a line, a very long line, of clansmen were marching towards Glenfinnan. Cameron of Lochiel had given in to the remarkably persuasive talents of the young prince and finally arrived with over 800 of his clansmen. Even if Prince Charles had shown no outward signs of despondency, he must have breathed a mighty sigh of relief. Later still, Ranald, son of the chief of the Clanranald, arrived with another 250 men. They had been delayed following a skirmish with British Government forces near Spean Bridge in what was effectively the first battle of the 1745 Rebellion. They had even brought along prisoners taken at Spean Bridge; among them, British Army Captain Swettenham, who had to look on helplessly as this sizeable Jacobite army formed in front of him. Charles insisted the prisoners were treated well, not least because he would have been well aware of the propaganda opportunity this would provide when they were released. To some extent, he was right, as it was reported that the captain, when ordered to give an eyewitness account direct to King George II, stated that Prince Charles Edward Stuart was "as fine a figure and as clever a prince as could be". As the celebrations got underway, assisted by brandy the prince had brought along, the aging Marquis of Tullibardine took to a small hill overlooking the head of Loch Shiel, and there he raised the standard of King James III of England, VIII of Scotland. The prince then read out a formal proclamation stating that his father had appointed him as prince regent and followed through with a rousing speech that was probably delivered in a clear-cut English accent which, we can be sure, would have been completely lost on many of the gathered clansmen who spoke only in the Gaelic language. Whether they understood him or not, Prince Charles Edward Stuart had that intangible quality we call charisma, and there is plenty evidence to suggest that few could resist his charm. Even Cameron of Lochiel, whose clansmen now formed the majority in this initial Jacobite army, had been warned by his own brother not to meet with the prince, as his resolve not to join the rebellion would fall apart upon such a meeting – as indeed it did.

During my lifetime, I can only think of two major politicians with such levels of charisma, and that has got to be Prime Minister Tony Blair and President Bill Clinton. I have seen Tony Blair at work on occasions when we provided transport for supporting staff during visits he made to the Highlands at the height of his premiership, and it left me in no doubt about his remarkable political talents. Unfortunately, I have never been in that privileged position with the former USA president. However, I have to mention a situation involving my late friend and colleague George Thompson, who worked with us for many years. George's only daughter lives in California, so he and his wife would spend the winter months over there. Politically, I have to suggest that his views were slightly to the right of Genghis Khan, so it must have made for some interesting conversations, as I understand that his daughter and her husband were confirmed Democrats and fervent supporters of President Bill Clinton. George most certainly was not, and given his strong ties to the USA, we were well used to his diatribes against the Clinton administration and, of course, the Blair administration in the UK at that time. Being the absolute professional that he was, George would keep his views to himself when touring during the summer with our American guests, so it didn't really matter, and among ourselves, it was an irrelevance since, as friends, there were times when we simply agreed to disagree. I cannot remember what year it would have been when I received an email from a government agency looking to book a minivan to transport people around the Dornoch area for a couple of days, but I recall thinking it must be American guests, as we tend to use the term "people carrier" rather than "minivan" in the UK. It turned out to be American Secret Service agents, so clearly they were to be there for the protection of a principal guest. Although this was not exactly an everyday occurrence, we were covering a lot of government-related work during that period, so it was not particularly unusual, and subsequently, neither I nor George, who I had allocated to go to Dornoch, thought a great deal about it. This was during the crazy busy summer months, so it was a week or two before I caught up with George and got the chance to ask him if the principal on the Dornoch job had been someone we might have heard of. "Oh yes," said George. "On the first day, I was told that the boss likes to meet people who are working with them, so that morning, on the first tee of Dornoch Golf Course, I shook the hand of former president Bill Clinton." Seeing the slight hint of panic on my face, he immediately followed up with, "Don't worry, I didn't say anything out of turn. In fact, I have to say that Mr Clinton is one of the finest gentlemen I have ever met." Now, I doubt if they exchanged more than a few words during a very brief period, but I can honestly tell you that my ultra-right-wing friend George Thompson sang the praises of the former president for the rest of his days. That is real charisma of the kind that few leading figures throughout history have shared, though I suspect that Prince Charles Edward Stuart may have been one who did.

The persuasive talents of the young prince, loyalty to the Stuart dynasty, reversal of the Act of Union, and for some, a desire to see a resurgence of the Catholic Faith were undoubtedly the significant factors in the 1745 Jacobite Rebellion, but we also need to recognise the very basic motives of self-interest and self-survival. Any clan chiefs who chose the losing side would almost certainly risk the confiscation of their lands and possessions followed by a lifetime in exile or, if captured, execution. While many of them turned out for the Jacobite cause, there were others who either tacitly, or actively, supported the government, as well as those who simply tried to remain sitting on the fence. A few tried the approach of having a foot in both camps, where the chief himself might have appeared to be loyal to the government, but he would also send one or more of his sons to fight on the Jacobite side. For ordinary clansmen, the decision to fight was all too often based on a threat by their chief to make them and their families homeless if they refused, and in some cases they were literally looking down the barrel of a gun. Whatever their motivation, those who gathered at Glenfinnan were now part of a Jacobite rebel army and would do what was asked of them, whatever the consequences. John Ramsay of Ochtertyre, who was about nine years old in 1745, wrote many years later:

"It was perhaps one of the most innocent and orderly hosts ever seen, considering they had no discipline and not much pay."

Whatever the fears of his Scottish subjects, Prince Charles was convinced that more and more would join his cause. He was completely unperturbed when informed that George II, and the British Government, had put a price on his head of £30,000. His immediate reaction was to put an identical price on the head of George, Elector of Hanover, who, of course, he refused to call a king.

After some discussion, it was decided not to march north from Glenfinnan to Inverness, where support from the Fraser Chief Lord Lovat and other Highland clans had been indicated, but instead they chose to take a more southerly route, with the intention of taking the City of Edinburgh early in the campaign. By following the more difficult route via Corryarrock, they avoided a confrontation with the British Army forces of General Cope at Dalwhinnie, though by all accounts, that was not exactly the plan, as Prince Charles was keen to bring about such a confrontation. By the 31st of August, they had reached Blair Castle, where the prince spent the night, though today there is no obvious "Prince's Room" to suggest where he may have slept, as the family had extremely divided loyalties and would not have sought to advertise the fact that he stayed within their castle walls.

By early September, they had reached Perth, where the prince was met by Lord George Murray, who had commanded Jacobite forces during the 1715 Rebellion. Lord George had been a highly respected leader during the 1715 and 1719 rebellions, though he was later pardoned on condition that he turn his back on the Jacobite cause and swear his allegiance to the House of Hanover – which he duly did in 1739. At the beginning of the 1745 Rebellion, he was still on the government payroll as Sheriff Deputy for Perthshire and, in the weeks before the prince arrived in Perth, Lord George had actually met with General Cope to discuss the situation. Nobody was quite sure which way he would turn, but there was a general feeling that his sympathies probably still lay with the Jacobite cause, so hopes were high that he would choose to join them, as his military ability would be a very real and much-needed asset. Following his meeting with the prince, it was clear that Lord George Murray was still a Jacobite who would again fight for the cause he had always truly believed in, even though other members of his family, including his brother, the 2nd Duke of Atholl, were to remain as firm government supporters. Although he was unquestionably an asset to the Jacobite army, there were lingering doubts about his ultimate loyalty, especially among the prince's Irish advisors, as they simply did not trust Lord George, though it has to be said that his intransigence and arrogance did not exactly endear him to many of his colleagues. The prince, however, clearly respected Lord George and, for the most part, was willing to trust his judgement though there is little to suggest that this respect was on a mutual basis, as from the outset, it was clear that the strong-willed Lord George Murray was going to clash with a Stuart prince who believed in his own absolute authority. The prince had intended that Lord George would share command with James Drummond, the Duke of Perth, who had already been appointed as the Jacobite commander. However, the experienced Lord George made it abundantly clear that he was not willing to share duties with the younger, inexperienced duke. Fortunately for the prince, the Duke of Perth was an amiable diplomat who stood down in favour of Lord George, as indeed he would do again later in the campaign since conflict between the prince and his general was to become an unfortunate feature of the 1745 Rebellion. With the obvious benefit of hindsight, we can see that suspicions relating to Lord George Murray's loyalty were misplaced and this undoubtedly created unnecessary friction within senior ranks of the Jacobite army. Whatever the character flaws of Lord George Murray, he was an experienced, highly competent general. The Jacobite cause needed him; they knew it, and so did he.

Having received news of promised French and Spanish assistance, the prince now headed for Edinburgh via Stirling and Linlithgow, where he spent several quiet, contemplative hours at the palace that had been home to many of his ancestors, before spending the night of the 15th of September in a house nearby. As the Jacobite army drew closer to Edinburgh, they were met by a deputation who had come out from the city seeking assurances from the prince that no harm would come to the capital and its inhabitants, though in reality, they knew that General Cope and his army would soon reach the city, so they were probably playing for time. The prince was equally aware of the arrival of Cope's forces and knew he had to take action, so a group of around 800 Jacobites, led by Cameron of Lochiel, prepared to storm the city walls. As the deputation returned to give their report to the city's magistrates a small group of Lochiel's men pushed through the gates before the city guards could close them behind the arriving carriages of the deputation. As regular troops retreated to Edinburgh Castle, and local militia stood down, the city was taken without any resistance. Shortly after, Prince Charles Edward Stuart, resplendent in Stuart tartan, entered the city in triumph to loud cheering among local inhabitants. Such apparently spontaneous enthusiasm may have been genuine but was just as likely inspired by basic instincts of self-preservation, not to mention a degree of curiosity, as not many in Edinburgh were genuine Jacobite supporters. From the wealthiest to the poorest citizen, few, if any, had much in common with kilt-wearing, tartan-clad Highlanders, who were generally looked upon with great suspicion. There was undoubtedly a sense of relief that the marauding clansmen did not quite live up to city residents' pre-conceived notions, as discipline within Jacobite forces ensured a relatively peaceful occupation. After the initial shock, I think it might be fair to say that some sections of Edinburgh's population were actually quite taken by the dashing young prince, and that was certainly true among many women within the city, whether or not they were supportive of the Jacobite cause. The term "Bonnie Prince Charlie" came into regular use and simply related to his good looks and charismatic personality. On the day of their arrival in the city, a proclamation was read out at the Market Cross declaring James VIII as the rightful King of Scotland whilst the prince settled in at Holyrood Palace. He was the first royal Stuart to enter this palace since his grandfather James VII of Scotland, II of England, so it is hardly surprising that large crowds gathered hoping to see the prince. The Stuarts had indeed "come home".

The following morning, the prince heard the news he had been longing for: General Cope had landed at Dunbar, just south of Edinburgh. At last, he would confront the enemy. A council of war was immediately convened at Holyrood, where the prince declared, to the horror of those present, that he would personally lead at the head of the Jacobite army as they marched out to meet General Cope. It took his advisors some time to get through to the young, headstrong Prince Charles Edward Stuart that the rebellion would almost certainly be over if anything should happen to him, so it was not a risk they could contemplate. The prince reluctantly agreed. On the 20th of September, slightly inland from Port Seton, the two armies were within sight of each other, but it was clear that Cope's army had the best position, as an attack from any direction would likely result in heavy casualties, so it was extremely fortuitous when Lord George was approached by a local landowner who knew a safe way through the marshland on one side of Cope's encampment. This surprise element gave the Jacobite side a distinct advantage when the battle got underway early on the 21st of September. In less than fifteen minutes, it was clearly over, as government forces turned and fled, including General Cope, who now rode for Berwick-on-Tweed as fast as his horse could carry him. He was described at the time as the "first general to bring news of his own defeat", though presumably not to his face. Prince Charles, to his credit, immediately ordered that the killing should stop and that all those injured on the field must receive equal and immediate medical assistance. As he rightly pointed out, they were all his father's subjects.

Not surprisingly, this victory was a massive morale booster for the Jacobite army, but it was also a turning point, as unity of purpose was now open to question. For many clan chiefs and their clansmen, this was pretty much mission accomplished, as they had taken back control of Scotland, but for Charles it was just the beginning, as the throne of England would be the real prize. During the prince's daily council meetings, divisions among his advisors became more and more obvious though even those who agreed with the plan to march on London had to accept the delay, as too many clansmen had drifted off to their homes after the victory at Prestonpans. Any further progression would have to be put off until they returned or new recruits could be found. Subsequently, Prince Charles Edward Stuart was to hold court in Edinburgh for almost eight weeks, but he remained optimistic, as he was now surer than ever that, following his spectacular victory, French help would soon be on its way. At that point in time, he was right, as the French were indeed planning an attack on England. However, the Hanoverians were also on the move, with the aging Field Marshal Wade moving towards Scotland on the east side of the country, and King George II's own son, the Duke of Cumberland, having returned from Flanders with another large force, would soon be in pursuit of Jacobite forces. Ever anxious to confront the enemy, Charles wanted to march his Jacobite army to Newcastle for direct engagement with General Wade's forces, but once again, he had to submit to the will of General George Murray, who insisted they avoid any such confrontation by taking the westerly route towards Carlisle. If the population of Edinburgh had been anxious about the arrival of the Jacobite army, it is fair to say that people in English towns and villages were terrified, as they believed stories they had heard about the savages from the north who pillaged, raped, murdered, and ate children. You can only imagine the relief when they discovered that the Highlanders, who may have looked pretty scary, were at least human. Due to strict discipline imposed on the Jacobite army, even looting was kept to a minimum.

By the time Field Marshal Wade received news that the Jacobite army was marching towards Carlisle, the winter snow had arrived, so he was stuck at Newcastle and could do nothing. Wade's extensive knowledge of the Highlands and its people would certainly have been an asset for the British Government, but he was in his seventies now and, by his own admission, tired and worn out, so it is tempting to suggest that he might actually have been relieved that the weather intervened. Not so for Prince Charles, as, again, he was to be denied an opportunity to engage with the enemy. As for the City of Carlisle, they had no choice but to raise the white flag and surrender to the Jacobite army. The prince caused unnecessary problems by appointing the Duke of

Perth to accept the surrender of the city, which was something of a slap in the face for General George Murray, who was, after all, the senior commander. General Murray was furious and sent a letter of resignation to the prince which, to everyone's amazement, was accepted. Once again, the diplomatic skills of the Duke of Perth were required, as he made it clear he was willing to accept a lower position in order that the prince and his general could back down from this disastrous personal confrontation. It has often been forgotten that the Duke of Perth, to his great credit, was more ready than most to put the cause ahead of personal ambition. He was from a prominent Catholic family but very likely recognised the argument that it would have sent the wrong message for him to be seen as the person accepting the city's surrender, considering the prince and his father had given assurances of religious tolerance that a Stuart restoration would not bring a return to Catholic dominance.

Once again, the prince's Jacobite army was reluctant to go further and justified this by highlighting the fact that very few in England were joining the cause. However, by pointing to letters he had been receiving promising support, the ever-optimistic Prince Charles was still able to exert his remarkable powers of persuasion, so the march south continued. Their arrival in Manchester was something of a high point, as the general population seemed to be genuinely welcoming and, for the first time, a significant number of recruits came forward. The prince gave this group of around 200 the somewhat unimaginative title of the Manchester Regiment. To allay any fears about pressing on beyond Manchester, the prince produced a letter from his brother, Prince Henry, stating that the French would invade on December 9th. It was what they needed to hear, so the Jacobite army continued south towards Macclesfield, where they were informed that King George II's son, the Duke of Cumberland, was nearby at the head of a large army. General George Murray was concerned that they would be seriously outnumbered, so he decided to set up a subterfuge by briefly marching a contingent west towards Wales. Cumberland was duped and marched off in the wrong direction, allowing the Jacobite army to continue south.

On 4 December 1745, Prince Charles Edward entered the town of Derby and was now little more than a hundred miles away from the City of London. When news of the Jacobite advance reached them, the city was consumed by panic, with shops closing their doors and merchants withdrawing money from banks before escaping to the country. Even King George II was said to be preparing to escape by sea, though to be fair, that was more likely to have been Jacobite propaganda, or even wishful thinking. Meanwhile in Derby, Jacobite soldiers were jubilant, as was Prince Charles, though his council of war had serious reservations. When he met with them the following morning, the prince was clearly excited and ready to work out the plan for marching upon the City of London but found, to his utter dismay, that General George Murray and several others were planning the complete opposite. Most agreed that, without the anticipated Jacobite rising in the south, they were now significantly out of their depth. They pressed Charles to produce the letters he claimed to have received pledging support from English Jacobites, but he couldn't for one simple reason – they did not exist. Towards the end of the meeting,

General George Murray summed up the situation by stating that they were all willing to die for the Stuart cause, and that is precisely what they would do if they were to continue. They had no choice but to retreat as soon as possible to Scotland and continue the fight from there until such time as they had greater support. Prince Charles was the only one who did not agree and later admitted, "I could not prevail upon one single person to support me." As he departed from the final meeting of his war council in Derby, he declared that he was accountable only to God and his father and would therefore cease to ask for, or accept, any advice. He could barely contain his rage as he descended into a monumental sulk. Who was right and who was wrong about the decision to retreat from Derby will probably be debated forever more and will go down as one of the great "what ifs" of the Jacobite cause. The prince was well aware that the Jacobite army alone could not complete the task, but he also knew that France was preparing to invade. Whilst it was true that English Jacobites were not exactly flocking to the cause, he was convinced that latent support would quickly emerge when the tide was seen to turn. Maybe he was right. Could it be that his own leaders, not least the highly respected General Lord George Murray, actually let him down at the crucial moment? If there had been proper coordination, better communication, and greater trust between the prince and his Jacobite leaders, it may well have turned out quite differently. Much of what we know about the events at Derby come from reports by such people as Lord George Murray and Lord Elcho who, with the best will in the world, were by then caught up in the blame game, making it all the more difficult for us to understand what really happened. The campaign was far from over, but the decision to retreat from Derby was the beginning of the end.

Early on Friday the 6th of December, or "Black Friday" as it came to be known among Jacobites, the retreat began though it is quite likely that most among the ordinary clansmen were initially unaware of the direction they were now travelling in. As daylight arrived, they began to see familiar landmarks they had previously passed, and morale plummeted as the bitter truth dawned on them. Many, like their prince, had been spoiling for a fight which they would now be denied. The prince no longer marched at the head of his army; instead, it was Lord George Murray who led this dejected force as rapidly as possible to the Scottish border, as he knew all too well that the Duke of Cumberland was very close behind with a large army, though fortunately for the Jacobite army, the threat of a French invasion delayed his movement away from the London area. By the time the Jacobites were back in Carlisle, the prince's black mood had started to lift, as he convinced himself that, with French help on the way, this was no more than a temporary setback. The prince was so confident of imminent French support, he now insisted on a garrison being left at Carlisle Castle till such time as they could be relieved. This was very much against the advice of Lord George and others within his war council, but he had, of course, made it very clear that he was not willing to listen to them anyway. The Manchester Regiment volunteered, and tragically, though not surprisingly, Lord George was right, as shortly after the Jacobite army departed from Carlisle, it was overrun by Cumberland's forces, after which many of the Jacobites left behind were executed or sentenced to be transported to the West Indies. A Jacobite officer by the name of James Johnstone, who had refused to obey an order to stay behind as part of that garrison, declared he "would never be a victim by choice". I mention him, as I would like to think this eminently sensible gentleman might have been one of my ancestors. By the time this news reached the prince, he was in Glasgow and was doubtless genuinely horrified to hear of the fate of those he had ordered to remain at Carlisle, but he never admitted that he had been wrong.

On the 3rd of January, the prince left Glasgow for Bannockburn House near Stirling, where he awaited the imminent arrival of Lord John Drummond with significant reinforcements. Lord John was the exiled brother of the Duke of Perth. It was at Bannockburn House that he first met Clementina Walkinshaw, a niece of the house's owner, Sir Hugh Paterson. Prince Charles was immediately taken with the sophisticated and graceful Clementina, who had been named after his own mother, Clementina Sobieski, and from the outset, they became more than mere friends. Every good story requires a love interest!

Life for Prince Charles was also taking a turn for the better in other ways, as Lord John Drummond had finally arrived with reinforcement that now brought the Jacobite forces up to the remarkable strength of around 9,000. As was so often the case with the 1745 Rebellion, this good news was offset by bad news, as French support had dramatically faded when they heard about the Jacobite retreat from Derby. For now at least, the prince was blissfully unaware that all plans for a

French invasion of England had been cancelled. His priorities were Stirling Castle and a return to the City of Edinburgh, but neither would be easy. The government garrison at Stirling was going to put up a vigorous defence, and General Henry Hawley, who had replaced Field Marshal Wade, had arrived in Edinburgh. As usual, the prince was spoiling for a fight and, without consulting his war council, decided they should march towards Edinburgh to confront Hawley's forces. Lord George was furious at this lack of consultation and immediately sent one of his forthright letters to the prince and, given the response, Lord George had clearly been even more undiplomatic than normal. The prince's reply included the following: "When I came to Scotland, I knew well enough what I was to expect from my enemies, but I little foresaw what I met with from my friends." The Jacobite army did not march upon Edinburgh. However, a week later, General Hawley had moved his forces to Falkirk, and the prince, this time with the agreement of Lord George, headed his Jacobite army out to meet them.

The Battle of Falkirk commenced on 17 January 1745. It was a victory for the Jacobite army and that was almost entirely due to the skill of their General Lord George Murray, who was able to instil such discipline in those close to him that they held their ground till the enemy was almost upon them before opening fire. Within less than half an hour, government forces were in retreat. Unfortunately, discipline within the main body of the Jacobite army was distinctly lacking, as various units headed in different directions, causing chaos and confusion that resulted in them being unable to pursue the enemy. It was certainly a victory, but it did little to improve morale or unity within the prince's war council. Once again, to his credit, Prince Charles went back to the battlefield to personally oversee the burial of the fifty Jacobites who had been killed, as well as those who died on the government side, though they numbered closer to 500. As seemed to be the case after each major battle, Jacobite clansmen dispersed for a time, with those who could heading for home. Most would return, but it did mean a delay in any future military movement, which in the eyes of the prince would be to now take the fight to the approaching Duke of Cumberland. However, Lord George Murray and several clan chiefs had other ideas. Any thoughts of capturing Stirling Castle had to be abandoned and they should now retreat further north, at least until the arrival of spring weather. The prince did everything in his power to persuade them otherwise, but by now no one was listening. Perhaps in his heart, he was beginning to see the end of his dream as he declared:

> *"I know I have an army I cannot command any further than the chief officers please, and therefore, if you are resolved upon it, I must yield, but I take God to witness that it is with the greatest reluctance that I wash my hands of the fatal consequences."*

On the 1st of February, the Jacobite army started out for the north. This time, they split into two main groups, with Lord George and Lord John Drummond taking their section by a coastal route via Aberdeen and the prince leading the main body of the clans up through the Highlands. For both, as well as smaller separate groups, the destination was Inverness.

By mid-February, the prince was close to Inverness and, on the night of the 16th, dined at Moy Hall as a guest of Lady Anne Mackintosh, whose husband, the Mackintosh clan chief, was actually on the government side, serving as an officer in the Black Watch Regiment. When this news reached Colonel John Campbell, Lord Loudoun, who was commanding government forces based in Inverness, he immediately headed for Moy Hall at the head of a significant number of his troops – possibly up to 1,500. Fortunately for the prince and Lady Anne, a sympathiser had rushed ahead of this force to warn of their imminent arrival, so the Prince was able to escape. Primarily as a delay tactic to give the prince more time, Lady Anne ordered her servant staff, possibly twelve or less, to create a diversion by spreading out and making as much noise as possible. In the pitch dark of the late evening, they lined up and started to run back and forth shouting random commands. In between, they took turn in firing shots at the government army marching towards them. The shouting and banging coming from various directions did more than simply cause a diversion, as Lord Loudoun and his men were convinced that they were facing the entire Jacobite army, so hastily retreated. The "Rout of Moy", as it came to be known, helped cement the growing reputation of Lady Anne Mackintosh, who had already helped to raise an army of almost 2,000 men to fight for the prince. Though, of course, at that time it would have been inconceivable for her to have actually led troops into battle, she did, with good reason, come to be known as Colonel Anne. As you might expect, she was placed under arrest when this was all over, but bearing in mind her husband's position as both the chief of the Clan

Mackintosh and, more importantly, a captain in the British Army, we should not be surprised that after a matter of weeks, she was released into the "custody" of her husband. There has been speculation ever since that both husband and wife were working together in order to ensure they held on to their land by having a foot in both camps. We will never know for sure, but the very fact that they appeared to have a perfectly normal and happy marriage thereafter does perhaps provide a clue?

Two days later, the bulk of Lord Loudoun's forces left Inverness and retreated further north. On that same day, the victorious Prince Charles marched into the town where, shortly after, he was joined by Lord George Murray. The prince took up residence variably between the Inverness Town House of the Dowager Lady Mackintosh and Culloden House, just outside the town, which belonged to Duncan Forbes, the President of the Court of Session and Scotland's senior law officer. Forbes was the most influential government figure in the Highlands and had been instrumental in persuading many Highland clan chiefs to stay loyal to the British Government. Prince Charles, now settled in Duncan Forbes's home at Culloden, appeared to regain some of his optimism as attempts were now made to consolidate Jacobite control in the Highlands. Forces were sent out in pursuit of Lord Loudoun, whose army was eventually scattered throughout the northern Highlands, as Loudoun himself, along with Lord President Forbes and the clan chief Macleod of Macleod headed for the Isle of Skye. The Jacobite cause had not been entirely abandoned by France and Spain, as ships with arms and cash were still trying to get through; occasionally with some success, so there was a lingering sense of hope. However, the fact remained that supplies were running low, and the prince was rapidly running out of funds whilst the Duke of Cumberland's well fed, well-armed, well-trained, and very much larger force was inexorably drawing nearer. By the 15th of April, they had reached the small town of Nairn, barely fifteen miles from Inverness.

Lord George Murray was among those who strongly supported the idea of a surprise night-time attack on the British forces' encampment at Nairn in the hope that they could replicate their success at Prestonpans, where similar tactics had been used. They were also aware that the 15th of April was the Duke of Cumberland's twenty-fifth birthday and believed that resulting celebrations among his troops might render them slightly less alert than normal. The Jacobite army split into two, one led by Lord George and the other by the Duke of Perth, with each following a different route in order to create as little disturbance as possible and avoid any detection that might give advance warning to the enemy. Both sections planned to arrive in Nairn by 2 a.m. in order to launch the attack on what they anticipated would be unprepared British forces, but the plan went badly wrong. Jacobite troops, who were already exhausted through lack of food supplies, struggled in the rough terrain and frequently became disorientated in the pitch black of night, resulting in progress that was painfully slow. By 2 a.m., Lord George's section was still a few miles short of Nairn and, having been informed that both the Duke of Perth and the Prince were well behind, he began to doubt if they would all reach their target before dawn, with the inevitable result that the element of surprise would be lost. It could not have been an easy decision, but Lord George now concluded that they had no choice but to turn back. The confusion that night is reflected in the varying reports of what actually happened, but it would appear the prince was unaware of Lord George's decision and had almost reached Cumberland's forces before the news reached him and he too had no choice but to turn back. By the time all sections of the Jacobite army had returned to the area around Culloden House, they simply collapsed with exhaustion and slept wherever they lay down. Meanwhile, Cumberland's troops were by now fully aware of the aborted attack and, despite the thoughts of Jacobite leaders relating to celebrations surrounding the Duke's birthday, they were well rested and ready for action. Being a regular British soldier during that period was far from an easy life, as they were subject to extreme discipline, with floggings being a fairly regular occurrence and even executions were by no means unusual. General Hawley, who had commanded British forces at the Battle of Falkirk, was known as "Hangman Hawley" due to the number of his own men he had executed for disobeying orders. Although Cumberland would undoubtedly have enforced discipline, he appears to have used his power more wisely and clearly took more interest in his men's welfare than most of his contemporaries. As a result, he inspired a significant level of genuine respect and loyalty.

By 5 a.m., Cumberland's army was on the march and ready for battle. When the news reached Lord George, the clansmen were rudely awakened from their all too brief slumber. A few pleaded with the prince to retreat, but most, including Lord George, knew this was not really an option. Some men were so exhausted they slept through the noise of the rousing pipes and drums whilst others had wandered to search for food, so the Jacobite army of around 5,000 that marched towards Culloden Moor was well below their full strength. Jacobite leaders were divided when it came to the best location, but time was not on their side, so for better or worse, their forces lined up on the rough, wet ground of the moor, where, facing eastward, they were blasted by a bitter, stinging wind. Although many were now running on pure adrenalin, they stood resolute in the drizzling sleet and rain as they watched the advancing British forces arrive and form in front of them. Shortly after midday, the first shot was fired from the Jacobite side as they attempted to take out British cannons, but it was quickly responded to by devastating firepower that quickly silenced the Jacobites' large guns and killed many in their frontline. The clans held position, as they had done at Falkirk, in the expectation that the government line would come forward, but as more and more fell under constant fire, the order to charge was finally given and a large swathe of the Jacobite ranks charged forward to engage in hand-to-hand combat. British soldiers were ready, as Cumberland had drilled his men in a way that would counter the famous Highland charge. Amid the subsequent carnage, it very quickly became clear that they stood little chance against the might of this well-trained British army. They had no choice but to fall back. Within about forty-five minutes, it was over, as Jacobite forces fled the field with the British Army in pursuit. Prince Charles Edward Stuart had to be persuaded to leave the field and escape. It is often quoted that at this point, Lord Elcho, who commanded the elite Lifeguard Cavalry, shouted at the prince, "There you go, you damned cowardly Italian."

Although by now, in common with many Scottish Jacobite leaders, Elcho had little respect left for the prince, he knew him well enough to be aware that he was no coward. Diaries kept by Elcho actually provide us with a great deal of information relating to events throughout the 1745 Rebellion, so it is interesting to note that he personally makes no reference to this. I think we can safely conclude that this quote attributed to him probably ranks among many "famous words" that were never actually spoken.

Within a few days, a large number had regrouped at Ruthven Barracks to await orders from their prince. Estimates of how many vary significantly from 1,000 to 3,000, but either way, there would have been a large number, as it was not only survivors from the battle who arrived there but also many who had not even made it to Culloden. Lord George Murray also arrived and, along with everyone else, heard the message from the prince which thanked them for all they had done but then stated that each man should now save themselves as best they could. The rebellion was over.

I have to admit that I have done little more than provide a basic outline of the 1745 Jacobite Rebellion and there are many important figures I have not even mentioned. Had you not already known, you will by now have realised that it is a massive subject that really needs to be fully explored by reading one of the many well-researched books that deal with it in a much more detailed manner. To me, and many others, a book published back in 1963 simply called *Culloden*, written by John Prebble, is still the one that tells the best story. I say story because Prebble was a great storyteller and you quickly become engrossed in his narrative, which concentrates heavily, and somewhat sympathetically, on regular clansmen and British soldiers on either side of the conflict. He is fairly even-handed and generally relates to the leaders on both sides with equal disdain. However, it does not really tell you a great deal about the biggest question of all – why? For that reason, I would also recommend you take a look at more recent works on this subject by historians such as Murray Pittock. The Jacobite rebellions of 1715 and 1745 were momentous events in Scottish, English, Irish, Welsh, and indeed European history. The more you study the subject the more, I can almost guarantee, you will want to know, though as always, you will come across many different opinions based on many different interpretations.

Popular culture has definitely contributed to recently increased interest in Scottish history and that is certainly true of Jacobitism. We only have to look at the "Outlander" novels and television series to see the effect it has had on an international audience. Closer to home though, there are other factors at play, including the political landscape in Scotland today, which to some extent is driven by a desire to reshape our history. The stuttering emergence of nationalism in the second half of the 20th Century became a roar within a few decades and today that nationalism utterly dominates Scottish politics.

22

Prince Charles Edward Stuart

When the history of the 1745 Rebellion is told, the position of Prince Charles Edward Stuart rarely attracts much in the way of sympathy from the time he landed on Eriskay through to his departure from the battlefield on Culloden Moor. We tend to look upon him during that period as a reckless young man who was way too full of his own self-importance, so yes, it is very tempting to portray him as a pompous egotist who brought nothing but devastation to his ancestral homeland and I confess there have been times when I have used similar terms during conversations with touring guests. However, I have to mitigate this by again pointing to the differing aims and objectives of many Jacobite supporters; some were Catholic, some were Protestant, some supported the union of 1707, though most wanted that union to be reversed. Among clan chiefs, there were many who, with good historical reason, did not trust the Stuarts but quite simply had greater contempt for the Hanoverian "usurpers". Even allowing for the legendary charm and charisma of Prince Charles Edward Stuart, we have to acknowledge that, given so many competing aims, he faced an uphill struggle throughout, so who could blame him for falling back on his father's, not to mention his own, "unquestionable" monarchical authority. The romanticised "Bonnie Prince Charlie" really came to the fore between the 16th of April and 20th of September 1746 when he was a fugitive in the Scottish Highlands. It is during this period that he appears to have cemented his appeal among the people of Scotland, if not, indeed, all of the United Kingdom. Perhaps it comes from our instinctive desire to support the underdog.

While Lord George Murray, the Duke of Perth, his brother Lord John Drummond, and a number of surviving clan chiefs headed south to Ruthven Barracks at Newtonmore, the prince and his ever-loyal Irish advisors, Sir Thomas Sherridan and Colonel John O' Sullivan (two of the original Seven Men of Moidart), headed west. It has been suggested that, in the face of defeat, Sherridan and O' Sullivan feared that some Highlanders close to the prince could no longer be fully trusted. Even Lord Elcho's Lifeguard Regiment, who had effectively been acting as the prince's personal protection squad, had been ordered to leave them and head for Ruthven. Given the confused situation at that point in time, they probably were anxious about the possibility of betrayal and, of course, there was still the matter of the very substantial price that remained on the prince's head. Equally, they may simply have concluded that a smaller group could travel more quickly and avoid capture. As they travelled west, they stopped at a house where the elderly Simon Fraser, Lord Lovat, was hiding out and he apparently urged the prince not to give up by reminding him of how many times his great ancestor Robert the Bruce had been defeated but still came back to ultimately win a glorious victory. Sherridan and O' Sullivan were not impressed and extricated the prince as quickly as possible before he could succumb to the charms of the "Old Fox", as Lovat was known. Lord Lovat was indeed cunning, and long relied on his ability to face in both directions to save him, but not this time. He was captured, tried for treason, and subsequently beheaded – the last person in the United Kingdom to be executed in this manner.

With Lord Loudoun's troops now returning from Skye and government soldiers spreading out from Inverness, it was going to be all the more difficult to stay out of sight, so the decision was made that the prince, accompanied by a very small number, should head for the Western Isles. The hope was that a French ship could gain access to them easier from there, so it is somewhat ironic that, only a few days after the prince departed for the islands, two French ships, who were searching for him, did actually arrive close to Arisaig. They had to depart without the prince but were able to rescue a group that included the Duke of Perth, Lord John Drummond, and Lord Elcho. The prince and his small entourage were now heading north in the Hebridean Islands to the town of Stornoway, on the Isle of Lewis, where they hoped to hire a boat to take them to France. Unfortunately for them, the people of Stornoway wanted nothing to do with the prince and effectively chased them out of the town. Understandably, Prince Charles was upset by this and was later described as having raged with anger, though in fairness, almost every other report about his time in hiding portrays him as generally good-humoured, polite, gracious, and genuinely grateful for all help given to him. Whatever meal was presented to him, however simple, he would eat with enthusiasm as though it was the finest food he had ever consumed, and he would sleep in whatever conditions were made available without ever complaining. No doubt such stories were often embellished in the retelling, but the consistency of the narrative does indicate a basic truth. Despite his positive demeanour, the prince did appear to be physically ailing and it became obvious that he was suffering from dysentery, so copious amounts of brandy were prescribed as the chosen remedy. We can only assume that he was very sick, as he was soon consuming a bottle of brandy every day. Those who met him were amazed at his ability to drink so much yet remain relatively sober, though it probably did cure his dysentery.

The most famous of all the stories relating to the prince's months in hiding involve a young lady by the name of Flora Macdonald. Her stepfather, Hugh Macdonald of Armadale, was in command of militia sent to the South Uist Islands to search for the Young Pretender, but we can safely say that Captain Macdonald was a Jacobite sympathiser, and he had no intention of actually capturing the prince, who was now being looked after in the relative comfort of a house belonging to the Clanranald chief, Ranald Macdonald. As intelligence reports were gathered, it was becoming increasingly clear to the Duke of Cumberland that Prince Charles Edward Stuart was very likely being hidden somewhere in the Western Isles, so the search could no longer be left to a small militia. Close to 2,000 British soldiers now arrived (many of whom were Highland clansmen) to search for the prince, and a virtual blockade was set up round the islands, meaning that nobody could leave for the mainland without showing a passport. With no hope of a French ship gaining access to these shores, it appeared to be no more than a matter of time before they would find the prince. Someone had to come up with a plan and that someone was Neil MacEachain (Neil Macdonald), a tutor in the Clanranald household, who had become the prince's guide. Neil was aware that Captain Hugh Macdonald's stepdaughter, Flora Macdonald, was on the Isle of Uist visiting her brother and would shortly be returning to her home on the Isle of Skye, so with Captain Macdonald's agreement, he approached Flora with a somewhat crazy plan. When she returned to Skye, Neil suggested that she should be accompanied by him, along with a female servant: Prince Charles Edward Stuart in disguise. Flora's initial response was to suggest that the idea was absolutely absurd, and she wanted nothing to do with it, but after some persuasion, she agreed to at least meet the prince. We cannot know if Flora was taken with the charm he evidently still possessed or if she simply took pity upon the thin, gaunt, and clearly exhausted young man she met, but either way, she agreed to help. Three passports, surreptitiously arranged by her stepfather Captain Macdonald, were made out for Flora Macdonald, Neil MacEachain, and Betty Burke, her Irish servant. With the help of Lady Clanranald, suitable female clothing was altered for the very tall prince, and a boat was hired for the journey to Skye. It would be a full week before everything was in place for the journey and throughout government troops were drawing ever closer to where the prince was hiding, so when the time came, the fear and excitement was mixed with relief. The prince was highly amused and caused some anxiety among those around him through his apparent inability to take the matter seriously. Flora had to persuade him not to have a pistol hidden in his underskirt, as it would almost certainly give them away if he were searched. His reaction was fairly understandable: "Indeed, Miss, if we shall happen to meet with any that will go so narrowly to work in searching as what you mean, they will certainly discover me at any rate." On the evening of 27 June 1746, Flora Macdonald, Neil MacEachain, and the somewhat odd figure of Betty Burke walked down to the harbour, boarded the boat, and set sail. Somehow, they got away with it. More than a hundred years later, their journey would be immortalised in the 'Skye Boat Song' which more recently has been reworded as the *Outlander* theme song.

Speed bonnie boat like a bird on the wing
Onward the sailor's cry
Carry the lad that's born to be king
Over the sea to Skye

The prince would spend many more weeks as a fugitive, during which time he had to be constantly on the move to avoid detection. Despite the many deprivations he suffered, there is every indication that he continued to bear them with courage, dignity, and good humour. After a spell on the islands of Skye and Raasay, he returned to the mainland and again hid out in the areas around Glenmoriston and Moidart, all the time waiting for news of a French rescue ship. His constant movement took him into the Lochaber area, where he met up with Cameron of Lochiel, who was hiding out close to his family home at

Achnacarry. Whilst there, he received the long-awaited news that a ship had successfully entered Loch nan Uamh, where he had been dropped off the year before. On 20 September 1746, this ship sailed for France with Prince Charles Edward Stuart and Cameron of Lochiel among those on board.

During his five months as a fugitive, the prince liked, wherever possible, to leave a memento with anyone who had given him assistance and that supposedly includes an "elixir" recipe he left with Skye man John Mackinnon, who had been a captain in the Jacobite army. Basically, it was a brandy-based concoction, but the Mackinnons substituted this for whisky and for many years the results stayed purely within the family until the late 1800s when it was passed on to the then owners of the Broadford Hotel on Skye, who produced it for local consumption. A hotel client, clearly enjoying the drink, made the following comment in Gaelic: "*An dram buidheach*", which in English comes out as "the drink that satisfies", and from this the more anglicised name of Drambuie came into existence, though it was another Mackinnon who later set up the Drambuie Liqueur Company in the City of Edinburgh. I suspect the story may well have been "enhanced" for marketing purposes, but who could blame them. The most frequent item left by the prince appears to have been a lock of his hair, as can quickly be established by visiting museums and various historic homes throughout Scotland. During a trip where we visited several of these places, one of my guests rather astutely suggested that the poor man must have been bald by the time he finally left Scotland.

Initially, the prince was feted as a hero upon his return to

France, where he retained contact with many surviving Jacobite leaders who joined him there in exile. The notable exception was Lord George Murray, who had escaped to the Netherlands and now made it abundantly clear that he wanted nothing more to do with Prince Charles Edward Stuart; at that point a feeling that was, by all accounts, entirely mutual. Although the euphoria of his successful escape buoyed the Prince for a time, he soon realised that the situation had changed and the prospect of any meaningful French commitment to the Jacobite cause was, very obviously, receding. Perhaps more importantly, the prince himself had changed, as he had been visibly affected, both physically and mentally, by the whole experience. His fondness for alcohol was now closer to a dependency that was becoming increasingly difficult to hide, and he frequently became an embarrassment to those around him. In common with many alcoholics, everyone was to blame but himself and, with this, his charm and charisma slowly deserted him as he began to trust fewer and fewer people who, in turn, no longer trusted him. He was furious with his younger brother Prince Henry, who effectively gave up his place in line to the throne when he became a cardinal in the Roman Catholic Church. Charles's anger was perhaps understandable, as he feared this would undermine the guarantee both he and his father James, the Old Pretender, had given that they would convert to the Church of England if the Stuart dynasty was restored. He was equally angry, and not a little frustrated, that his father appeared to approve of Prince Henry's decision to become Cardinal York. In 1750, he even took the gamble of travelling to London so that he could be seen to take communion in an Anglican church, though the visit was so low key, few ever heard about it. It is hard to imagine the British Government being unaware of Prince Charles Edward Stuart's presence in London, but they probably made the wise decision to simply let him come and go without any intervention in order to ensure the visit remained secret and subsequently of little benefit to the Jacobite cause.

In 1748, Louis XV of France was under diplomatic pressure to banish the Young Pretender to the British throne from French territory. When Louis finally bowed to that pressure, Prince Charles Edward Stuart reluctantly departed from Paris, but rather than head to Rome to be with his father James III, the Old Pretender, he headed for the Netherlands.

The once charming, gentlemanly Prince Charles had a number of mistresses, including at one point his married cousin, the French Duchess of Montbazon, but his relationships never lasted due to his increasingly abusive nature when drinking. He would have been in his mid-thirties when he met up with Clementina Walkinshaw again, who he had first met at Bannockburn House near Stirling in 1746. No one seems to be sure of the exact circumstances though there was some speculation that Clementina was a Hanoverian spy, so their secret meeting in Paris may have included little or no element of coincidence. Either way, they shared their lives for some time and had a child together. Eventually, his abusive manner was too much for Clementina, so she left him, taking their daughter, six-year-old Charlotte, with her.

The Old Pretender died in January 1766, so Prince Charles Edward Stuart, in the eyes of his dwindling Jacobite supporters, became Charles III. A few years later, when Charles was fifty years old, a marriage was arranged to the German Princess Louise of Stolberg, with the obvious hope that he would yet produce a legitimate heir. It was a union doomed to failure though it was Louise's arguably understandable infidelity that ultimately led to a formal separation. In later years, he was reconciled with his daughter Charlotte, who was with him when he died in January 1788 at the age of sixty-seven. Despite Charles's best efforts, Charlotte could never be recognised as the legitimate heir, so it passed to his brother Henry, Cardinal York, who, despite his church status, went on to style himself as Henry IX though he never really pressed any claim to the British throne. When Henry died in 1807, his will stated that the Jacobite claim should pass to his friend and relative Charles Emmanuel Savoy though he, nor any subsequent member of that line, ever pressed that claim. In reality, the Stuart line was at an end, as was the Jacobite cause. Despite everything that had gone before, the monument sitting on top of the tomb in St Peter's in Rome, containing the remains of James III, Prince Charles, and Prince Henry, was actually paid for by the Hanoverian King George IV of Britain.

Jacobite supporters in England were both Catholic and Episcopalian, as indeed was the case in Scotland where, surprisingly, the cause was supported by a few Presbyterians who were motivated by a desire to see the end of the 1707 Act of Union. So yes, religion was important, but as previously mentioned, it was by no means the only issue. The Glorious Revolution of 1688, that led to each of the subsequent Jacobite rebellions, set off more than one bandwagon, with each being joined by groups who would not always seek to travel in exactly the same direction. That was arguably truer in Scotland than other parts of Britain, so when it reached a conclusion in 1746, it was the people living in the Scottish Highlands who would suffer the devastating consequences. This was not a Welsh conflict, an Irish conflict, an English conflict, or a Scottish conflict; this was a British conflict, and the solution would be imposed by a British Government.

23

After Culloden

The summary execution of Jacobite prisoners when the Duke of Cumberland captured Carlisle Castle gave an indication of things to come, but nobody could have been prepared for the murderous onslaught that would be unleashed upon the people of the Highlands following the Jacobite defeat at Culloden. While Prince Charles Edward Stuart, along with many Jacobite leaders, escaped to a life of exile in continental Europe, it would for the most part be ordinary citizens who would suffer the vengeful wrath of the Hanoverian Prince William Augustus, Duke of Cumberland. With very good reason, Cumberland was referred to as "the Butcher" since he was determined to spare no quarter in battle and no mercy in victory. To him, it appeared to be personal and, taking full advantage of his unique position as the favourite son of King George II, he could, and did, act in a manner that arguably no other commander could or would have done. When Duncan Forbes, who was Lord President of the Scottish Court of Session, returned to his home at Culloden House, his polite request that the army of His Highness, Prince William, Duke of Cumberland, should observe the laws of the country was curtly dismissed. There is little doubt that officers and soldiers in the British Army vigorously perpetrated atrocities that could only be classed as war crimes; though many were guilty of such acts, the fact that they took their lead, and orders, from Cumberland cannot be ignored.

At Prestonpans and Falkirk, Prince Charles Edward Stuart, son of the Stuart Pretender to the throne, ensured that casualties on the opposing side received medical attention. He personally supervised teams sent out to bury the dead on both sides and demanded that prisoners were treated with dignity. The contrast with his distant cousin, the Duke of Cumberland, son of the reigning Hanoverian monarch, could not have been starker. On Cumberland's direct orders, no medical assistance was allowed to be given to the wounded and dying who lay on Culloden battlefield, and no friends or relatives were given access to bury their dead. Those who were taken prisoner were held in various locations in Inverness, including the Old High Church, which served as a makeshift prison. A number of prisoners, following the briefest of trials, were immediately executed. Some faced their executioner as they stood in front of a gravestone in the churchyard. Many more died during their imprisonment. It would be easy to fill these pages with eyewitness accounts from the period detailing the many atrocities, though as always, we have to be conscious of the propaganda element which almost inevitably set in from an early stage and doubtless grew as the years went by. However, it has to be said that even if we were to discount many such reports, the damning evidence would still be utterly overwhelming. The following is a reported statement by James Bradshaw, an English Jacobite, immediately before his execution:

"After the Battle of Culloden, I had the misfortune to fall into the hands of the most ungenerous enemy that I believe ever assumed the name of a soldier, I mean the pretended Duke of Cumberland, and those under his command, whose inhumanity exceeded anything I could have imagined. I was put into one of the Scotch kirks together with a great number of wounded prisoners who were stripped naked and then left to die of their wounds without the least assistance; and though we had a surgeon of our own, a prisoner in the same place, yet he was not permitted to dress their wounds, but his instruments were taken from him on purpose to prevent it. In consequence of this, many expired in the utmost agony."

No excuse can ever be found for the barbaric treatment meted out to the people of the Highlands in the aftermath of Culloden, nor can Scotland hide behind the idea that it was a vicious act of English revenge, because we cannot escape from the simple and unedifying fact that many of the men serving in government regiments were Scots and, indeed, some were Highlanders. They were British soldiers serving in the British Army.

Within less than a month of the battle, Cumberland had moved to Fort Augustus and from there his soldiers rampaged through the Jacobite territories of Lochiel, Glengarry, Keppoch, and Cluny, among others. No Jacobite was to be taken prisoner, as in the eyes of the Duke of Cumberland, they were traitors who had no right to life. Women and children who were allowed to live had their homes burnt and livestock removed; in some cases, even their clothing was taken as loot, so they stood little chance of survival. The cattle, seen as the spoils of war, were taken south by drovers to be sold to the highest bidder. In 1747, legislation was brought forward banning the wearing of tartan, banning teaching of the Gaelic language, banning bagpipes, and less surprisingly, banning the carrying of weapons. This affected all Highlanders whether or not they had been Jacobite supporters and can only be seen as enforced cultural and social engineering, by an occupying force that was intent upon "civilising" the Highlands. The British Government were determined that there would never be another Jacobite uprising. It could certainly be argued that the abolition of Heritable Jurisdiction that was also passed by the Westminster Parliament in 1746 brought more uniformed law to the Highlands, as it removed power from clan chiefs who up to that point had pretty much been the primary source of law within their own territory, but it also served to further erode the tribal culture of Highland clans. Most important, from a government point of view, it removed the right of any clan chief to raise a private clan army. Many of these clan chiefs had already started to make the transition from tribal leader to straightforward landowner, though the suppression of the Highlands after Culloden undoubtedly accelerated that process. Many more years would pass before it would dawn on ordinary Highlanders that their clan chiefs' priorities were now more about extracting money from their land assets than any traditional commitment they once had to their clan's people – the people who actually lived on that land. With few exceptions, loyalty became a one-way street.

It can take time to convince some of my guests that Jacobitism was a movement existing in all parts of Great Britain as well as areas throughout Europe and was most definitely not confined to the Scottish Highlands. This brings the frequent and perfectly understandable question: "Why, in that case, were the atrocities that took place after Culloden, and the subsequent oppression of the people, restricted to the Highlands?" There is no denying that is basically true. Brutal acts of retribution against Jacobite supporters in the south of Scotland did occur, but the violent suppression that took place in the Highlands was on a completely different level. Despite the broad spectrum of aims and objectives among Jacobite supporters in different geographical areas, we have to acknowledge the perception, at that time, of the Scottish Highlands as a primary source of Jacobitism since, after all, this and every previous Jacobite rebellion did start in the Highlands. I think it is fair to say that the feudal system, though in decline throughout most of Great Britain, still dominated the lives of ordinary Highlanders whose primary loyalty was to their clan chief. In many ways, it was even more specific in the Highlands, as it could often be based on blood ties among senior family members, in addition to powerful tribal loyalties. This allowed for the mobilisation of clansmen at very short notice, so Jacobite-supporting chiefs could still raise large and fairly instant armies. Even allowing for the fact that Highlanders were never more than part, and not always the largest part, of Jacobite forces, you can begin to see why the British Government was concerned about Jacobite roots in the Highlands. The culture and basic lifestyle of ordinary clansmen produced great warriors whose reputation could strike fear in their enemy before they even reached the field of battle, so again, the Highland area was seen as a potential breeding ground for any Jacobite army.

Although a few clan chiefs and senior members of their family had connections to the south, most ordinary clanspeople lived very simple lives and rarely moved far from where they were born. Their way of life was certainly different from most people living in England and, indeed, the Scottish Lowlands at that time. They certainly looked upon "backward" Highlanders as little more than savages and that is how most British soldiers would have seen them. Whether it was a view shared by army commanders or one they would simply utilise we cannot be certain, but we do know that by de-humanising Highlanders they could somehow justify their orders to carry out the most horrendous atrocities. I am not sure we can ever fully explain the whys of the aftermath of the Battle of Culloden, as there are times when it is just too difficult to conjure up the empathy required to truly understand some situations.

The entire Jacobite period has been subject to significant revision in more recent years and that cannot be a bad thing since the traditional view of Culloden as the last great battle between Scotland and England, ending in English domination, is fundamentally wrong, but unfortunately, it is one that still persists. Many of our American guests in particular see this in colonial terms since it is, perhaps not surprisingly, easier for them to understand events in that context. However, Scotland never was a colony. Scotland was actually a coloniser, even before the Battle of Culloden, and then to a much greater extent after Culloden, when it became a more integrated part of the British Empire. The "romanticised" view of the Jacobite cause, Jacobite rebellions, the Battle of Culloden, and its aftermath comes largely from the fictionalised retelling of Scottish history during the early 19th Century and to some extent that view is still perpetuated by modern fictional drama.

What would have happened if Jacobite forces had marched on from Derby to London? What if the 1745 Jacobite Rebellion had succeeded? What would have become of Scotland? We know that many, though certainly not all, Jacobite leaders were fighting to reverse the 1707 Act of Union between Scotland and England, and we also know that Prince Charles Edward Stuart and his father, who would have been James III, did indicate that they would support such a policy, so it is possible, perhaps even likely, that Scotland would have returned to the status of an independent nation, though how independent is something that could be open to debate. Given the absolutist style of monarchy still favoured by the Stuarts, might Scotland have indeed ended up as a colony in an English Empire? A Jacobite victory would certainly have altered the dynamics of European politics, with inevitable international consequences. Would French support that allowed for the creation of the United States of America have been forthcoming in such circumstances? Would the USA exist today, at least in its current form? Such questions do appear to be fairly ludicrous, but we sometimes have to look at the hypothetical consequences of alternative results in order to fully appreciate the importance of events and situations. It certainly brings home to my guests the very real significance of the final Jacobite rebellion.

As for the Duke of Cumberland, you will not be surprised to hear that he was lauded as a conquering hero when he returned south. This was also true in parts of southern Scotland, where he was given the honour of the Freedom of the City of Glasgow.

The General Assembly of the Church of Scotland sitting in Edinburgh expressed their gratitude to the Duke, and he was made honorary Chancellor at Aberdeen and St Andrews University. In England, and London in particular, he received a rapturous welcome and was seen as their great saviour. 'See the Conquering Hero Come' was written by Handel in his honour. At that stage, Prince William Augustus, Duke of Cumberland, could do no wrong. However, as more and more reports of atrocities in the Scottish Highlands began to leak out, the clearly appropriate "title" of "the Butcher Cumberland" came into more widespread use. In 1757, when commanding allied forces during the Seven Years' War, he suffered humiliation and a significant fall from grace when he failed to defend his family homeland of Hanover from French attack. Cumberland died in London in 1765 when he was only forty-four years old and has not been remembered with great affection in any part of the British Isles. In Scotland, and certainly the Scottish Highlands, he will always be remembered with utter contempt.

Many of my touring guests want to know what happened to Flora Macdonald after she helped Prince Charles Edward Stuart escape from South Uist to the Isle of Skye. Did he write to her, did they keep in touch? Unfortunately, I have to shatter any romantic thoughts, as Flora was simply one of many who helped the prince during his time as a fugitive in Scotland, though it has to be said that her actions showed great courage. Unfortunately for Flora, it was not long before she came to the attention of government officials and she was subsequently arrested for assisting the prince's escape. Having survived on a grim prison ship that transported her to London, it would appear that her imprisonment there was slightly less arduous. This may have been influenced by public support she was already gaining among those who saw her as a truly heroic figure. Given her growing reputation, it is not surprising that she was among those granted amnesty in 1747 and she was free to return to her native Isle of Skye. In 1750, Flora married Alan Macdonald, the eldest son of Macdonald of Kingsburgh, and they settled on the island, where they raised a family of seven. When the celebrated writer Dr Johnson toured in the Highlands, he met with Flora and described her in such glowing terms that it further enhanced her reputation. However, her fame did not bring any material wealth, so like many others at that time, Flora, her husband, and two of her sons chose to emigrate to colonial territories in North Carolina, where they became highly respected members of the community. However, everything was to change once again for Flora and her family when America declared its independence. Alan Macdonald had previously served as a captain in the British Army, so having sworn an oath to the Hanoverian monarchy, it is hardly surprising that he would again take up arms on the side of the British, alongside both their sons. Flora played her part by going round the area seeking volunteers to likewise fight on the British side. In 1776, Alan and both sons were taken prisoner at the Battle of Moore's Creek Bridge and, a year later, Flora and her family were among loyalists on the losing side who had their property confiscated. Following the release of her husband and sons, they spent a brief spell in Halifax, Nova Scotia, before returning to their homeland in 1779. Though their original Skye property was now occupied by other members of the family, Flora and Alan's later years were reasonably comfortable due to the significant earning of their third son, John, who acquired his fortune in India. The people of Britain never lost their affection for the heroic Flora Macdonald and when she died in 1790, the Isle of Skye witnessed the largest funeral it had ever seen as thousands came to pay their respects.

24

Scotland Re-Invented

When you walk down Princes Street in Edinburgh, you cannot miss the Scott Monument. Like many famous buildings and monuments, it initially attracted a great deal of criticism though it is now readily accepted as one of the city's most famous landmarks. This ornate Gothic structure commemorates Sir Walter Scott, who, through his fictionalised writing on Scottish history, did more than anyone to re-invent the image of Scotland. He romanticised Highland warriors and brought his version of their lifestyle into a new, albeit false, perception of historic Scottish culture. During the height of Scott's popularity, the image of a tartan-clad, kilted, bagpipe-playing Highlander became synonymous with all parts of Scotland, though he was well aware that it would have been completely alien to the ancestors of Lowland Scots. Sir Walter was a proud and patriotic Scotsman as well as being a staunch Unionist, so considered himself to be both Scottish and British. Bitterly felt consequences of the 1745 Jacobite Rebellion still lingered as part of very recent history at that time, so you can perhaps understand his motivation in trying to give the people of Scotland a clear, unifying identity within the context of the United

Kingdom, but without the context of Scottish nationalism; it would of course be a somewhat fictionalised identity. It was Sir Walter who found the Scottish Crown Jewels (the Honours of Scotland) in a deep basement in Edinburgh Castle, where they had been "mislaid" for over 100 years, though in truth, they had been forgotten about following the Act of Union in 1707. This, and the fact that George IV was a fan of Scott's first novel *Waverly*, gave him the opportunity to invite the King to Edinburgh for a royal visit that would be stage-managed by Sir Walter, thereby allowing him to showcase this new version of his beloved homeland. Given that no reigning monarch had set foot in Scotland for 172 years (the last to have done so being Charles II), this would be no easy task, but nobody could have been better prepared than Sir Walter Scott.

George IV was by no means a popular king in England, mostly due to his overly extravagant, not to mention debauched, lifestyle. In later years, his voracious appetite for food and alcohol was beginning to take its toll on his health as he became ever more obese. On 15 August 1822, King George IV arrived in Edinburgh, and there is no question that he was warmly welcomed by the people of the city. In the coming days, he would attend numerous events that were carefully choreographed by Sir Walter to show the distinctive culture of Scotland; a Scotland that was, nevertheless, a loyal part of the United Kingdom. It was, of course, a Highland culture that would be on display or at least the version that Sir Walter chose to portray. He persuaded a number of Highland lairds to attend these events in their more traditional role of clan chief and, to emphasise this, they were to appear in full

Highland dress. Given that a number of these clan chiefs were now absentee landlords who spent little time in their family homelands, it is not surprising that many had no idea what the relevant tartan should be. I suspect the question: "What is our clan tartan?" was often followed up with, "Err, do we actually have a clan tartan?" Somehow, Scott managed to raise seven clan "regiments" including Campbells, Macdonnells, Sutherlands, Drummonds, and Macgregors to parade in front of the King in full Highland regalia. He was so successful that he actually had to turn down offers from other attending chiefs who were willing to bring a contingent from their clan. Since Sir Walter's own family were from the Borders, where tartan and kilts had never actually existed, he had a slight problem, as he obviously did not have a tartan himself. Fortunately, he remembered that his great-granny was a Campbell – problem solved. Outwith army regiments, tartan had really gone out of fashion, so the help of various experts was called upon, though the person that really saved the day was the army tailor and supplier George Hunter; a busy man who was also called upon to produce a kilt and full Highland regalia for the King. What else but Royal Stuart tartan could be chosen for King George IV, though flesh-coloured tights were added to his attire in order to protect the King's modesty. I am quite sure many of the great and good attending the events held in the King's honour would have readily told him how wonderful and handsome a figure he was dressed in the garments commonly worn by his loyal Scottish subjects. They would, of course, have been lying through their teeth – in every respect.

It is easy, very easy, to see the royal visit by George IV as something of a circus, with Sir Walter Scott as the ring-master, and we have to acknowledge that many contemporary commentators took that view, especially in relation to the King himself, who undoubtedly did look utterly ridiculous. However, we cannot deny it was an event that not only changed Scotland from within but also fundamentally changed the image of Scotland on a worldwide basis. Some might argue that it brought an end to the divide between the Highlands and the Lowlands, though as a native Highlander, I would argue that was not, and is still not, entirely true. However, it could certainly be suggested that Sir Walter Scott did manage to finally de-weaponise Jacobitism and turn it into an acceptable, benign concept, though we also have to acknowledge that this was during a period when Scotland was strongly committed to the union, so it no longer presented any kind of threat to England.

The "tartanisation" of Scotland continued throughout the 1800s and was turbo-boosted by Queen Victoria when she bought Balmoral Estate in Aberdeenshire and built Balmoral Castle in the area that came to be known as Royal Deeside. To this day, it is a favoured, if not the favourite, holiday retreat for the royal family, where they are frequently seen wearing tartan and kilts, though I am glad to say they do not look anywhere near as ludicrous as their ancestor George IV. Prince Charles, for one, is rarely seen in Scotland wearing anything other than a kilt and I must confess I have this image of him entering a phone box Superman-style as he approaches the Scottish border wearing a lounge suit, then suddenly emerging in the garb of a Highland chieftain. It is fair to say that romantic writers of the late 1700s and the first half of the 1800s, alongside Queen Victoria, really invented Scottish tourism, as through their influence, attitudes to the Scottish Highlands completely changed. No longer were the Highlands looked upon as barren, inhospitable lands full of strange backward people; they were now seen as dramatic, beautiful lands, full of romance. Having spent a lifetime in the modern tourism industry, I should perhaps be grateful to them all even if this was an image that bore no resemblance to the harsh reality of life for the people who lived in the Highlands at that time.

There were, of course, many others who contributed to the re-creation of Scotland's image during the early 1800s though there are some we are ever so slightly reluctant to mention. This brings me to the Welsh brothers, John and Charles Allen, who travelled to Edinburgh to witness the extravagant visit by George IV. They were the sons of a fairly wealthy naval officer, and both were genuinely fascinated by Scottish Highland culture. When they changed their names to John Sobieski Stuart and Charles Edward Sobieski Stuart, it appeared that their interest was due to a connection, a very close connection, with the royal Stuart household. Bearing in mind that James Francis Stuart (James III) had married the daughter of King John Sobieski of Poland, there were many in Scotland's polite society who were ready, and perhaps more than willing, to believe they were the real thing, so chose to treat them accordingly. Lord Lovat, among many others, was so convinced he gave them a home on his estate near Beauly, where they held court and acted in a manner befitting royalty. In 1842, the brothers published what they claimed was an ancient document called *Vestiarium Scoticum* detailing a vast number of authentic tartans with both written detail and colour illustrations. Shortly after, they followed this with a further version under the title of *The Costumes of the Clans*. Now, if the upper classes of Scotland welcomed the "Sobieski Brothers", you can only imagine how happy tartan weavers and tailors must have been, especially when you consider that their books were printed round about the same time that Queen Victoria first fell in love with Scotland. However, it was not very long before an investigation by the equivalent of today's investigative journalists exposed the brothers as complete frauds, so for a time, they disappeared, but the work they produced did not disappear. They may well have been fantasists, but they were incredibly talented fantasists who produced remarkably detailed drawings for seventy-five clan tartans that Scotland's weavers were very, very reluctant to give up. The solution was to convince themselves, against all the obvious evidence, that the tartan illustrations in these books were based on authentic originals, so they could continue to use them, which they did, and their modern-day counterparts still do. About forty years ago, a friend persuaded her father, Arthur Varley, who was a master tailor and kiltmaker, to make a kilt for me in my Johnstone Clan tartan, which I can tell you is still in pristine condition, though for some reason, it is a little tight around the waist now. The Johnstone tartan used in that kilt is one of the many illustrated, and almost certainly invented, by the Welshmen, John and Charles Allen. I should also mention that my name simply means John's Town, whereas the other spelling, Johnson, not surprisingly, means Son of John. Two completely different names, but the same tartan is shared by both.

During conversations on the subject of kilts and tartan, some of my guests, quite rightly, challenge me on this by suggesting that tartan was in use long before the Sobieski brothers appeared on the scene and they are, of course, absolutely right. There were tartans already in existence relating to regions and, in some cases, names as well as those within the military. Equally, there is no doubt that many, including Prince Charles Edward Stuart, saw tartan as the Jacobite "uniform". Indeed, that is one of the reasons why a significant number among those who still had sympathies, albeit romantic sympathies, for the Jacobite cause badly wanted to believe that the Sobieski Stuarts were the real thing. When we talk about re-invention in relation to tartan, we are talking about the plethora of dubiously authentic versions created in the first half of the 19th Century.

While most people in Scotland have long since come to terms with an image that largely came about as a result of this early 19th Century re-invention, many are slightly embarrassed by the falsehood of that image and want to see the promotion of Scotland as the modern country it is today. Now, given the fact that I have spent a lifetime working in the tourism industry, I have to admit to a certain bias, but that does not stop me suggesting that we have a strong, powerful brand image that few countries in the world can match. Yes, there has been a significant degree of embellishment, but that is now part, though really a fairly small and entertaining part, of the total story of Scotland, so I have to ask: why we would now seek to completely abandon such a powerful image? During my early days as a driver/guide, I was fairly reluctant to dispel the myths of Scottish culture with my guests and, if I am going to be honest, this was partly down to lack of knowledge, but it is equally fair to say that attitudes were slightly different at that time. I think that on this, Scotland can actually have it both ways, which is a rare but great position to be in, though I suspect the debate will continue.

We have to be honest with our guests, though I have to admit that is not always easy when they have Scottish ancestral connections, as the very image we have projected with such great success can result in many within the Scottish diaspora viewing the land of their forefathers through what can only be truthfully described as rose-coloured glasses. During a short tour when I was travelling with a multi-generation family from Texas, the grandfather did not really feel up to walking round Edinburgh Castle when we were there on the last day of our trip, so I took him to a nearby coffee shop while the rest of the family enjoyed their castle visit. Given that they only had a few days in Scotland, he had mostly held back in favour of his grandchildren, as he specifically wanted them to learn as much as possible throughout the time we had together. As a result, I had not really had any lengthy conversations with him until we sat down to enjoy our coffee. Only then did I discover that this elderly Texan gentleman had Macleod ancestry going back many generations. His genuine sense of pride and, to some extent, sadness was obvious as he told me how his ancestors and clan chief had suffered during and after the Battle of Culloden. Now, the truth is that many Macleods did indeed fight on the Jacobite side at Culloden, but Norman Macleod of Macleod of Dunvegan, the 23rd clan chief, had resolutely refused to support the Jacobite cause. A few years previous to these events, he had been accused of conspiring in the kidnapping of ninety-six women and children from the Isle of Skye, including some of his own people, to then have them shipped out to the American colonies and sold as "indentured labourers", where each would have fetched a figure of around £3. This unbelievably cruel plan would have succeeded had the ship not been grounded off the coast of Ireland when all were rescued and eventually returned to their homes on Skye. Many believed that the surprise decision by the Macleod chief not to support the 1745 Rebellion was due to a pact he had made with the British Government, giving a guarantee that he would not support any future Jacobite uprising in return for an assurance that this sordid incident would not be investigated. It never was. Whether or not Norman Macleod of Macleod was involved, we cannot be absolutely sure, but it does not reflect well on his position as clan chief. I briefly wondered if I should relate that story to my new friend and kindred spirit, but ultimately I did, and I am glad to say that he was greatly fascinated rather than offended. Quite rightly, he still left Scotland as a proud, though hopefully better informed, member of the great Clan Macleod. Incidentally, I would have had to relay the same story had he been a Macdonald of Sleat (Skye), as their clan chief was also implicated.

A similar situation arose when I was driving with a couple from Skye to Glasgow. With impeccable timing, the lady mentioned that she really enjoyed the film *Rob Roy* with Liam Neeson in the lead role, as she had a distant Macgregor connection in her family. I say impeccable timing, as we were, at that very point, little more than a few miles from Balquhidder

Church, where Rob Roy Macgregor was supposedly buried. As we stood in that little churchyard, I began to elaborate on the real Rob Roy and how (as I previously mentioned) he was actually a nasty bit of work, a conman and thief who really could not be trusted. I immediately sensed this was not going down terribly well when she suggested that I was making it all up and basically slandering one of her ancestors. Even now, I am not entirely sure how serious she was, but as we returned to the car, her husband turned to me and said: "Jim, I have been married to her for forty years and, after what you have just told us, everything is starting to make a lot more sense." Hopefully, they made it to their forty-first anniversary.

People who have been to Balquhidder Church will be very surprised by the suggestion that Rob Roy was "supposedly" buried there since, after all, they stood in that churchyard beside a grave with a headstone that bears his name. Donald Maclaren, the present chief of the Maclaren clan, is of the firm belief that Rob Roy was actually buried in an unmarked grave several miles from Balquhidder, and resents the suggestion that he was buried in what the Maclaren's see as their territory. The Maclaren chief has even requested that this "false grave" should be exhumed in order to prove his point though, so far, his request has fallen on deaf ears. Rob Roy was undoubtedly laid to rest somewhere but, even now, the same cannot be said of this longstanding clan feud between the Maclarens and the Macgregors.

25

Georgian Period

One could hardly say that Britain looks back upon Georgian monarchs with any great enthusiasm, despite the remarkable changes and advances that occurred during the 116-year period of their rule. George I and George II had an uphill struggle to overcome their Germanic origins, so it might be fair to say that most people in Britain merely tolerated them as the only available option to the unwanted Catholic Stuart monarchy. To Jacobite supporters, they were foreign usurpers who had to be overthrown by whatever means necessary, but as we know, it was the Hanoverians who ultimately prevailed and, by the late 1700s, Jacobitism had faded as a lost cause, though it left an indelible mark on Scotland. When we use the terms "Georgian" and "Regency" we are, of course, referring to the period, whilst Hanoverian relates to the royal house and, specifically, to the origin of monarchs from that family line. In the context of Jacobitism, it is perhaps not surprising that the term Hanoverian is more frequently used than the more benign period reference. To add to this confusion, the latter part of the House of Hanover reign is referred to as the Regency period even though the actual Regency, on behalf of George III, lasted for only eleven years.

Direct power of monarchs had been in decline from the time of the installed Dutch king, William of Orange, and this was further re-enforced when the Hanoverian George I was likewise installed as the first of another new line of monarchs. Slowly but surely, more and more power was being transferred to Parliament. To a great extent, this suited both George I and II, partly because they had never actually ruled during a time of absolute monarchy, but also because they were frequently pre-occupied with continental European conflicts, so for the most part, they were quite content to leave domestic matters to Parliament. The major exception was the ever-present threat from the Jacobite cause though that too had a distinctive European element.

George III was only twenty-two years old when he ascended to the throne in September 1761 following the death of his grandfather George II and will forever be remembered as "Mad King George" and the "King who lost America". In fairness, neither description is particularly accurate. Over the years, almost all my American friends have suggested to me that it was excessive taxes imposed by the crazy George III that caused the American colonies to rebel and ultimately turn their back on monarchy. Whilst it would certainly be fair to say that he would have opposed American independence, it was Parliament that set taxation policy, not the King. He suffered two bouts of major mental health issues in 1788 and 1810 that, for a time, left him completely incapable of ruling, but in between times, he was very much in control, able to function normally and indeed successfully. George III was the first of the Hanoverian monarchs who was born in England and, as a result, was perhaps given his place more readily as a monarch of the Georgian period even if that does make the people of Britain sound just a touch xenophobic, though heaven forbid that I should ever suggest such a thing. Despite these known issues, he enjoyed periods of remarkable popularity during his long reign of fifty-nine years, though due to a complete breakdown of his mental health, he had not been fit to rule during the eleven years prior to his death in 1820. His son George Augustus, Prince of Wales, ruled as regent till his father's death when he became George IV in his own right though at no time would he ever equal his father's popularity.

When he was seventeen, George Augustus, then Prince of Wales, secretly married a twenty-three-year-old actress by the name of Mary Robinson and stayed with her for several years. Apart from the more obvious problem of her "lowly status", Mary was also a Catholic, so it is perhaps fortunate for Prince George that this marriage was never officially recognised. Following pressure from his family, not to mention pressure to pay off massive debts he had incurred due to his profligate lifestyle, George agreed to marry Caroline of Brunswick, the daughter of his aunt, though he was not remotely happy about it. He probably had good reason, as Caroline is reported to have been short, fat, and ugly, with no sense of personal hygiene. Nevertheless, they both did their duty and a daughter, Charlotte, was born in 1796, after which he told Caroline that he would have no further relations with her, so she could do what she wanted, and that is exactly what she did by having a number of affairs and generally indulging in a pretty scandalous lifestyle. Fortunately for the British establishment, Caroline spent most of her time overseas, but she was determined to re-emerge and take her rightful place as queen when her husband ascended to the throne as George IV; she even refused a "bribe" of £50,000 in return for a promise to stay out of the country. On the day of his coronation, Caroline arrived at Westminster Abbey and demanded to be allowed in, but the door was slammed shut. She returned to where she was staying and promptly wrote a letter to the King, who was still legally her husband, demanding that a date be fixed for her coronation as queen, which, of course, was never going to happen. She died only days later, and on her deathbed insisted that the following should be inscribed on her coffin: "Caroline the injured Queen of England". This sentiment was widely shared by the general public at that time, despite her obvious failings.

Charlotte, the daughter of George and Caroline, was brought up and educated with a view to her one day being the reigning Queen of Great Britain. She was, by all accounts, a difficult child and a rebellious teenager, but in 1816, the now twenty-year-old Charlotte agreed to marry Prince Leopold from the German house of Saxe-Coburg. Within a year, she was pregnant, and George IV was overjoyed at the news that he would now have a grandchild and additional heir. Sadly, after a long and difficult labour, Charlotte lost the child and, within days, she too died as a result of complications.

George IV died in June 1830 and having left no legitimate heirs, the throne went to his sixty-one-year-old brother, who became William IV. As with his brother, William was not a particularly popular king, but in fairness, it was never going to be easy for him to make his mark, coming to the throne so late in life. He did at least have a pretty clear idea regarding the limitations of a monarch since he stated: "I have my view on things, and I tell my ministers. If they do not adopt them, I cannot help it. I have done my duty." Though he reigned during the politically turbulent years of the Great Reform Bill, that would extend the voting franchise, he had one main ambition in his later years and that was quite simply to live long enough to ensure that his niece, Victoria, came of age to directly replace him as the reigning monarch. This was based on a hatred of his sister-in-law and Victoria's mother, the Duchess of Kent, along with her close ally, the decidedly dubious Sir John Conroy. William was determined that they would not be given the opportunity to act as regents for the young Victoria. William IV succeeded, as he died in 1837, exactly one month after Victoria's eighteenth birthday.

Although Victoria was from the Hanoverian line, she was not, unlike her predecessors, able to take on the title of Ruler of Hanover since, as a female, she was barred from that line of succession. The Hanoverian line really ended with William IV, as Victoria took the name of her husband Albert who, like Victoria's mother, was from the German family of Saxe-Coburg, so the House of Hanover now gave way to the House of Saxe-Coburg. And yes, you are right, Victoria and Albert were first cousins.

Although the hated 1707 Act of Union was in its infancy at the beginning of the Georgian period, it had come to be recognised as greatly beneficial to both Scotland and England by the time of the Regency, as thoughts increasingly turned away from internal conflict and turned instead to trade and industry.

The expanding British Empire brought great wealth to those at the top of society and created a middle class that would expand during the Industrial Revolution though it has to be said that it did little or nothing to improve the lives of those at the bottom of the heap, as all too frequently they were forced to swap their peasant lifestyle on the land for the drudgery of low-paid factory jobs and the misery of living in city slums. Massive leaps forward by scientists and engineers undoubtedly changed lives, as did the new ideas put forward by the great thinkers of the Scottish Enlightenment. Adam Smith, as the "father of economics", was, and still is, quoted by those on the right and left of politics even if today the capitalist system he inspired is under great strain.

During the Georgian, Regency, and Victorian periods, Britain became an industrial powerhouse and, through its dominance of the seas, a military superpower. As a partner, albeit junior partner, Scotland reaped its share of the rewards though, again, it has to be said that the wealth created was shared by very few. Nowhere was that more true than in the Scottish Highlands.

26

The Highland Clearances

The Jacobite rebellion in 1715 attracted significant support throughout the lowlands of Scotland and that was primarily a result of antagonism to the 1707 Act of Union. By the time of the 1745 Rebellion, such feelings had by no means disappeared, but they had dissipated, particularly in the major urban areas of Glasgow and Edinburgh, where a significant number now wanted nothing to do with the Jacobite cause. Whilst it is also true that many in the Scottish Highlands did not actually support the Jacobite cause, we have to acknowledge the number of fighting clansmen who did (mostly at the behest of their clan chief) and how this subsequently locked in a perception of the Highlands in general as a hotbed of Jacobitism. Scotland has always had and, as previously mentioned, still has a distinct north/south divide, which encouraged that perception and undoubtedly contributed to the lack of sympathy among southern dwellers towards their fellow countrymen in the Highlands during the atrocities perpetrated in the immediate aftermath of Culloden. The cities of Edinburgh and Glasgow were by then venturing into a new "enlightened" age and beginning to reap the rewards of the union, so it is perhaps not surprising that they would now seek to emphasise their Britishness. It is no coincidence that the New Town of Edinburgh, where construction started in the 1760s, should have very loyal-sounding street names such as Princes Street, George Street, Hanover Street, and Frederick Street.

For the Highlands of Scotland, it was a very different story. In the brutal aftermath of Culloden, Highlanders were struggling to re-assert their own identity, let alone one that was British, or even Scottish. The romanticised version of Highland culture peddled in the late 18th and early 19th Century was a world away from the harsh reality of life experienced by the people who actually lived there. The Scottish Enlightenment brought new ideas, and the Industrial Revolution created the first real wealth in some, albeit limited, areas of Scottish society, but for the people of the Highlands, these changes only added to their problems, as they were tenants of landowners whose primary focus would now be their own wealth creation. The days of the paternalistic clan chief were over, as they simply became landowners who sought to maximise income from their land holdings. Many now looked upon the people (often their own clan's people) as a barrier; a barrier that, if need be, would have to be removed. It is very tempting to suggest that this was entirely down to the draconian measures put in place following the Jacobite defeat at Culloden, as it did indeed bring about the destruction of the accepted clan structures that previously dominated the Highland way of life, but the "gentrification" of Highland clan chiefs was underway even before 1746. However, we cannot ignore the impact of the 1746 Heritable Jurisdiction Act which ultimately removed the right of a clan chief to raise a clan army, with the result that having a large number of potential fighting clansmen on his land was no longer relevant or desirable.

Emigration from the Scottish Highlands had begun long before the tragic events that followed the Battle of Culloden though it undoubtedly increased in the immediate aftermath. For a time, after 1746, people in the Highlands were effectively living under the oppression of military occupation and that would almost certainly have influenced some though the reality of ever-increasing rents for small pockets of land was clearly a strong incentive for people to seek an alternative life elsewhere. Initially, some landowners and clan chiefs were alarmed by this development and sought to find ways to stem the tide of emigration; not least because they required cheap labour for the growing kelp (seaweed used in the manufacture of soap and glass) industry that had been established on their shores. However, this was to change as new ideas of land management began to sweep across the Highlands. Large areas would now be let to comparatively wealthy farmers, often from the south, who would raise sheep on that land. In later years, vast areas of land would be let to very wealthy tenants for hunting, fishing, and shooting. There was, of course, an obstacle to such change, as that same land was already occupied by tens of thousands of tenants and sub-tenants whose families had lived there for generations.

Tacksmen, who were generally related to the clan chief, held areas of clan land, which they would let out to tenants who, in turn, would let out part of that land to sub-tenants. Although the clan chief was at the top of the tree when it came to a share of rents, that was not traditionally the main benefit of the land holding. What really mattered was the number of fighting men a tacksman could raise for his chief; power was derived from the size of a clan army, not from the land itself. However, clan chiefs now took complete ownership of the land that had previously been looked upon as belonging to the entire clan. Their power would now be based on how much money they could extract from that land as opposed to the number of fighting men, as the currency of people was replaced by the currency of cash. The driving force behind the Highland Clearances was this fundamental change in the balance of power combined with a rash enthusiasm for new economic trends that, intentionally or otherwise, encouraged a ruthless rush to riches.

As more and more smallholding tenants were driven off the land, the need for a tacksman class of middlemen ceased to exist, so they too had to leave, and often that meant moving to other areas in Scotland or, frequently, emigration. On occasions, these tacksmen would take whole villages of their tenants with them to start a new life elsewhere, though most of the poorest tenants were removed to crofts on relatively useless land near the coast, where they were expected to augment their existence with fishing, which they knew nothing of. Many of those who voluntarily left the land their families had lived on for generations did so for the simple reason that the new exorbitant rents being imposed meant starvation was the only alternative. For others, their removal was entirely as a result of force, so in reality, choice never entered the equation. The law was wholly on the side, often by the side, of the laird's estate factors and the men they employed to carry out the evictions.

At very short notice, whole townships of men, women, and children were turfed out of their homes and forced to leave the area forever. In many cases, they were literally dragged from their houses and the roofs would then be set on fire to ensure that they could not be re-occupied.

Among the worst and most notorious clearances were those from land in the north-east Highlands belonging to the Countess of Sutherland and her husband, the Marquis of Stafford (later the Duke and Duchess of Sutherland), where something like 15,000 people were evicted from their ancestral homeland. Whilst we can all understand and perhaps even sympathise with Highland landowners who were on the verge of bankruptcy, as some were, the same cannot be said of the majority and that most definitely included the Duke of Sutherland who, at the time, was one of the wealthiest men in Britain. In 1812, James Loch, an economist and lawyer, was appointed by the Countess of Sutherland as the estate manager. Loch saw it as his mission to "improve" his employer's estate regardless of the consequences for the people living on that land, though it is just possible that he believed his own rhetoric when he suggested that it was ultimately as much for their benefit as it was for the landowner. This approach was also followed by the Sutherland's estate factor, Patrick Sellar, who was himself a large tenant sheep farmer. His responsibilities included the removal of the estate's smallholding tenants – responsibilities he appeared to relish. Whatever qualities Sellar may or may not have had, there is ample evidence that he carried out his duties with a zeal that few others would match; to the extent that he was eventually accused of culpable homicide and brought to trial. In the summer of 1814, Sellar had been involved in the eviction of William Chisholm in Strathnaver, during which the roof of his family home was set on fire regardless of who might still be inside – as indeed was Chisholm's mother-in law, Margaret Mackay. She was rescued from the burning building by her daughter but died a few days later. Sellar clearly had a manner that readily created enemies, so it was not only those he callously evicted who were keen to see him in court. However, bearing in mind that the law was entirely on the side of landowners, it is hardly surprising that he was acquitted of all charges against him and, as you might imagine, it was a result that did nothing to help the ordinary people who were being driven from their homes. The verdict simply strengthened the hand of landowners. As for Patrick Sellar, despite having by then fallen out with both James Loch and the Countess of Sutherland, he continued to lease more and more of the cleared land and became a very successful and prosperous sheep farmer. The seemingly never-ending process of depopulating the Scottish Highlands continued.

When we talk about the Highland Clearances, it is impossible to ignore the role of the church at that time, as it was central to the lives of most Highlanders. Presbyterianism, brought by the Scottish Reformation, took much longer to find favour among Highland clan chiefs who were mostly, though not exclusively, Catholic or Episcopalian, so the destruction of the clan system that was implemented after Culloden may have created something of a vacuum in the lives of ordinary clans-people. Arguably, this was filled by the Presbyterian Church following numerous missions and religious revivals in areas within the Highlands. Whatever the reasons, Presbyterianism gained ever-increasing traction. Did the teaching of obedience within the church somehow help to fill a void? After Culloden, did the defeated and demoralised Highland people find some kind of solace in the fatalist doctrine of Presbyterianism? Nobody really knows the answer to these questions, but it does not stop us speculating. By the time of the Sutherland Clearances, the Church of Scotland dominated Christian worship throughout the Highlands, and that has often led to the question: why is it that Presbyterian church ministers appear to have done little or nothing to help their people? They have even been accused of siding with landowners on the basis that the landowner was their patron. Whilst it is possible, perhaps even likely, that many church ministers were indeed motivated by self-interest, it might be unfair to take that as a universal judgement since the very doctrine of the Presbyterian Church, the doctrine of divine providence, did not permit them to intervene and this would have been understood and meekly accepted by their congregations. Most landowners used the offices of the local church minister as a go-between when seeking to pass on removal instructions to their tenants, who frequently spoke only in the Gaelic language, whereas many ministers had at least some understanding of the language. Even if we assume that these ministers may have pleaded on behalf of their flock, they ultimately accepted the landowner's instruction and passed it on in the full expectation that there would be no resistance. Under no circumstances would they encourage, or ever condone, breaking the law. If this was God's will, they had to accept and obey. With the absolute backing of secular law and the interpreted backing of God's law, Highland landowners had carte blanche to act in whatever way they chose.

Although the fundamentals of Presbyterian doctrine never changed, there was widespread discontent with the continued system of patronage in that the political classes and landed gentry (basically one and the same) still claimed the right to appoint church ministers. This led to frequent splits within the church, as they formed into two main camps – moderates and evangelicals. The largest split, by far, came in 1843 when, as you will recall, almost half of the ministers in the General Assembly of the Church of Scotland walked out and formed what they called the Free Church of Scotland. This event was known as the Disruption and it came about because evangelicals within the Church of Scotland finally chose to take decisive action against patronage. Evangelical ministers and groups of Highland lay preachers known simply as "the Men" had been the primary, if not the only, religious leaders to vociferously speak out against the Highland Clearances, so it is no surprise that Highlanders, in vast numbers, immediately associated with the new Free Church.

Free Church ministers could not be accused of self-interest, as all church property remained with the moderate section of the Church of Scotland and, of course, their new church had for the most part burnt any bridges with Highland landowners. They had to raise funds and start from scratch in the hope that they might still find landowners who would allow Free Church buildings on their land, though for many years after the Disruption, their services were still being held in the open air. You could certainly argue that they had every right to claim the high moral ground though any such claim was tarnished only three years later when the famous anti-slavery activist Frederick Douglass visited Scotland. He spoke at a meeting in Dundee, where he denounced the leaders of the newly established Free Church for raising substantial funds to support their project among slave owners in the American South. As a result, they were for a time bombarded by abolitionists with the slogan of "Send back the money" – which they never did. The founders of the Free Church of Scotland were arguably living during a time when it was hard to find the high moral ground, let alone occupy it.

The period of the Clearances, or Improvements for any that may still take that point of view, stretched intermittently from the mid to late 1700s through to near the end of the 1800s. It is another topic where you can read many different versions about what really happened in terms of the process, attitudes, and motivation, so again, we ultimately have to make up our own minds. The first book I read on the subject was by John Prebble, with the straightforward title of *The Highland Clearances,* and as with his book on Culloden, it is a story well told. Another of the early books I read on the Clearances was *The Making of the Crofting Community* written by the eminent Scottish historian James Hunter. It is certainly one I would still recommend though I would also add in one of his more recent titles: *Set Adrift Upon the World. The Sutherland Clearances.* I try not to load down my guests with too many suggestions, but I frequently sense a desire for more authoritative information, and that is particularly the case among those with Scottish ancestral connections. At least we are now in the age of online shopping, so even my most enthusiastic guests no longer need to head home with seriously overweight luggage.

Jim Hunter has also had a successful career in public life and served as Chair of Highlands and Islands Enterprise in the early 2000s during a period when we provided car services for that government organisation. As a result, I travelled many enjoyable miles throughout Scotland in his company, but would you believe, I never once discussed his above-mentioned book, or indeed any of the others he subsequently wrote. In many ways, I now regret this, though I must admit I felt at the time that it would have been unprofessional for me to do so. Journeys with business or government clients were often done in relative silence, as one of the real benefits for people who are being driven is the fact that they can work undisturbed, and in Jim Hunter's case, that often meant long periods of quiet contemplation. There were, of course, times when we did have conversations and I particularly remember one early morning journey from his Highland home to Edinburgh when he wanted to know about my more frequent role as a driver/guide and, in particular, how my touring guests perceive Scotland. In the process, I mentioned a phrase I often use when travelling with our American guests and indeed one I have already used earlier in this book: "We don't do optimism in Scotland." In general terms, he agreed and then used it to form the basis of a memorable conversation about why that should be. Having read *The Making of the Crofting Community*, I was not surprised to discover his feeling that it may have more than a passing connection to generations of Scottish Presbyterian church ministers telling generations of Scottish people how worthless they were.

More recently, I read a fascinating book called *The Scottish Nation 1700–2007* written by Tom Devine, who is another of Scotland's leading historians. In the final chapter, he quotes from a presentation Jim Hunter gave to a Scottish Parliament Committee in 2004 in his capacity as Chair of Highlands and Islands Enterprise. It began: "We just don't do optimism... Once in Scotland we paid preachers pittances to tell us we were no bloody good. Now we pay press columnists big fees to do the same." This quote resonates so strongly I think I would have included it whatever, but upon realising my possible role as a sounding board that morning in 2004, it became irresistible. The quote goes on to say: "And to do so in defiance of the facts... saddling us in the process with an unremittingly pessimistic commentary." In *The Scottish Nation,* Tom Devine quotes other prominent Scots who have made similar comments regarding Scotland's lack of confidence as a nation and, not accepting that adherence to Calvinism was at the heart of the issue, he seeks answers elsewhere, though I need to emphasise context, as that particular debate related to Scotland's economic performance.

If large sections within Scotland's population are indeed reluctant to embrace optimism "in defiance of the facts", it might suggest that economic performance, good or bad, is not necessarily a deciding factor, so our historical attachment to Presbyterianism must surely remain in contention as a primary cause. However, it is possible that part of the answer does lie elsewhere. Could it be that Scottish attitudes have more to do with the junior role Scotland plays, and always has played, within the slightly dysfunctional family of countries geographically bonded together within the British Isles, regardless of any political union? Is our pessimistic approach a perverse defence mechanism to counter the permanent domination of "Big Brother England"? Within the family of the United Kingdom, is Scotland suffering from "second son syndrome"? Even if my touring guests do not put these questions in quite such blunt terms, they will occasionally put forward subtle suggestions along these lines. However uncomfortable it may be for a Scotsman to hear, they just might have a point. As a driver/guide, I have the privilege of seeing my own country through other people's eyes and, yes, that can mean I spend time countering our stereotypical image, but every now and then you hear a pre-conceived thought you cannot counter because it does actually have a ring of truth. I can feel a Robert Burns quote coming on: "O wad some Power the giftie gie us. To see oursels as ithers see us!"

27

Scotland and the United Kingdom Today

What about 21st Century Scotland? Is it true that the Scottish Highlands never fully recovered from the Highland Clearances? Is the church still important to people's everyday lives? How relevant is the monarchy to people living in Scotland today? What about this Scottish independence thing? These questions are not surprisingly in the minds of my guests following our numerous conversations on Scotland's past, though I confess they are not always the easiest to answer since they can often involve a degree of speculation as to what the future may hold. This is particularly the case when it comes to current Scottish politics and contemporary views on monarchy, so I will put that aside for now.

Significantly, in 1745, more than half of Scotland's population lived in the north of the country, whereas today less than a tenth of Scotland's 5.5 million inhabitants live in that region. When you also consider that vast swathes of land in the northern Highlands, where many people once lived, now form part of the last great wilderness areas in Europe, it is very tempting to agree that the Highlands of Scotland has indeed never recovered from the period of the Highland Clearances.

However, it may be equally fair to ask if the shift in population was entirely due to the Clearances, as the answer may well be slightly different. Escalating urbanisation in the 19th Century was certainly not exclusive to Scotland and, given the very poor-quality land that was occupied by too many people in some Highland areas, is it realistic to think that such high levels of population could have been sustained indefinitely? Although apologists for landowners at the time, and since, deny the term "Clearances" in favour of "Improvements", no one can doubt that it was a cruel policy, all too often pursued in a brutal manner for the benefit of the land-owning classes. How the "expendable" people who lived on that land were to survive thereafter was given little or no consideration. However, here comes the "but". Although this was a shameful period, we should perhaps not allow it to completely cloud our judgement, as it may well be that de-population of the Highlands was ultimately inevitable. I would be the first to admit that not everyone would agree on that, including some of my touring guests. In more recent years, both the United Kingdom Government and the European Union have introduced stimulus packages in an attempt to revitalise the Highland economy, so there are occasional hints of optimism among the people of the Highlands who, as mentioned already, are mostly pessimists by nature.

Questions regarding the power of the church in Scotland today are much easier to answer, as like almost everywhere else, it is an influence that is on the wane and has been increasingly so over the past fifty years. During the 2011 Census, around 60% of people in Scotland classed themselves as Christians, with 32% attaching themselves to the Protestant Church of Scotland and 16% to the Catholic Church. Other Christian groups accounted for 5% and non-Christian religions less than 3%. Clearly these figures are out of date, and I suspect that there will be significant changes when the next census figures are announced. Although, as mentioned, church leaders from both the Protestant and Catholic churches were very powerful voices in Scottish society up until fairly recently, their ability to influence Scottish politics has greatly diminished. At the risk of upsetting members of my own family, I have to suggest that much of the blame for this lies at the church's own door. We all know about the self-inflicted damage within the Catholic Church and despite very recent, albeit limited, attempts to "modernise" the Protestant Church, there is little doubt that the more rigid scriptural interpretation still adopted by certain sections is at best a problem for many people whilst for some it is an interpretation that is now just plain unacceptable.

In the current climate, there is another subject our guests are keen to know more about and that is, of course, Brexit; a subject that has dominated British politics for some time. Since the 2016 referendum, it has become even more of an obsession for all of the United Kingdom, though it might be fair to say that the original Brexit debate was primarily driven by England. However, the decision to leave the European Union may yet have implications for all of the United Kingdom, to the extent that its very existence may be threatened. I confess that I sometimes struggle to fully explain the motivation behind this decision, as I am not sure that all of the people who voted for leaving the EU did so for the same reasons, though we cannot ignore the very clear evidence that perceived issues relating to immigration were a major factor. Not long after the referendum, one of my American guests, perhaps paraphrasing President Trump, suggested that it was an attempt to "make Britain great again". I conceded that he might have a point, though if so, it would be in the context of a Britain that, even now, has not fully come to terms with the ending of its once vast empire. This is not a unique observation though it is one that may actually carry a grain of truth. No matter how divisive it has been, and it has been very divisive, a democratic decision was taken, so Britain and Northern Ireland need to, and doubtless will, make it work in some shape or form. Whether it ultimately turns out to be a good decision or a bad decision, only time will tell.

As recently as the 1960s – when I was a young pupil in a small country school – the British Empire, and the part Scotland played in that Empire, was still seen in a strongly positive light. We were taught to believe that the benign influence of Great Britain brought huge benefits to the people living in all parts of that Empire. In more recent times historians have, quite rightly, challenged such ideas. I have chosen to mention this in the context of Brexit because a majority of those living in the United Kingdom today continue to look upon the Empire as something to be proud of. You will not be surprised to hear that many of my guests have strong opinions on this subject and they are often keen to hear my thoughts as a Scotsman, and citizen of the United Kingdom. I confess that I do not find it to be the easiest of subjects as I can recognise there were some positives, but at the end of the day, the creation of an Empire is really about power, and the seemingly inevitable exploitation of that power. In that respect the British Empire was no different from any other throughout history. What about the use of this word "benign"? If it is used as a comparative term then, yes, it could be argued that it still has some relevance though it does not alter the fact that too many aspects of British rule, not least in Africa and India, cannot and should not be defended. I urge my guests to read *Empire. How Britain made the Modern World* by the British historian Niall Ferguson who is Professor of International History at Harvard University. It is a fascinating book though, as always, you may or may not agree with his conclusions.

28

Monarchy in the 21st Century. Why?

Given my numerous discussions with guests about the history of our monarchy, it is inevitable that at some point I hear: "I have a question" followed by "Why in this day and age does the United Kingdom still have a queen?" It's a really good question and one that is not always easy to answer, or I should perhaps say it is difficult to provide an answer that makes sense to a non-UK resident. Why do sane, sensible people frequently become irrationally deferential, almost to the point of being subservient, in the presence of royalty? Believe me, it does happen.

During the many years when we were the main provider of chauffeur-driven car services in the north of Scotland, you will not be surprised to hear that we had occasionally been involved with guests who fell into the rich and famous category. Personally, I like to think that that all our guests are VIPs, but sometimes we have to go along with apparent norms; to paraphrase George Orwell, "some are more important than others". As you will recall from previous chapters, we have also provided car services for local, Scottish, and national government agencies. This mostly related to high-ranking politicians, senior government officials, and visiting dignitaries but did occasionally involve us in royal visits within the Highland area. My colleagues and I, and anyone else in this business, will tell you that, in this type of situation, the principal concerned can very often be polite, pleasant, and generally a pleasure to deal with. However, the same cannot always be said of the team that surrounds them and, from experience, I have to say this can frequently become very apparent during a royal visit, particularly among local "organisers" who may be brought in to assist during a specific event. When the Queen visited Inverness in 2000, we were contacted by a Scottish Government department to provide a car for the First Minister of Scotland, as he was to be one of the main dignitaries to accompany her throughout the visit. In order to reduce the number of vehicles in the official convoy, local dignitaries, including the Provost (Mayor) of Inverness, would travel with the First Minister, so we provided a six-seat people carrier. In the days before the visit, I was in the south of Scotland touring with a family, but at that time, I was the only one among our small team of drivers who had the relevant security clearance, so the night before the royal visit, I had to dash back to Inverness to prepare the vehicle. The following morning, I picked up the First Minister and took him along to Inverness Town House, where he met up with the Provost. When we left the town house, they were joined by three others for the short journey to the helicopter pad at Raigmore Hospital, where the Queen and Prince Philip would be landing. The five men in my vehicle were all middle-aged and upward with many years of public service between them, but you did not need to be an expert in psychology to sense the nervous tension in the air. We arrived at the location a good forty-five minutes before the Queen's arrival, as did others, so my passengers got out and mingled with the main reception group. At that point, a cheerful, easy-going government official (who I had met before) came along to speak with all the drivers and to make sure we were lined up the way he wanted us to be. A police patrol car would be in the lead and that would be immediately followed by the Queen's Rolls Royce limousine. Behind the limousine was a Special Branch (security) car, followed by a people carrier with royal household staff, then me, and finally the car taking the Northern Police Chief Constable at the rear. It was a line of six vehicles, escorted by the same number of motorcycle police whose job it was to ensure the road ahead was kept clear. This type of convoy would sometimes travel at high speeds and, given how close together you need to drive, it could be quite exhilarating, not to mention a little scary. However, we had been given advance notice that the pace on this visit would be more sedate. Having ensured the vehicles were correctly positioned, I went to have a conversation with the Chief Constable's driver in the car behind me who, again, I knew well. We had barely uttered hello to each other when a senior police officer approached us both. This officer I had not met before, so I was unsure of his rank, but he was clearly someone used to giving orders, as he informed us, in no uncertain terms, that the vehicles were wrongly positioned; the Chief Constable's car should not be at the back of the line. We did as we were told and started to switch the vehicles round when, needless to say, the government official who originally lined us up spotted what we were doing and came straight across: "I am going to guess that someone told you to do this – who?" he asked. "One of my bosses," replied the Chief's driver. With a hint of a smile on his face, the official turned to us both and stated:

"The First Minister of Scotland outranks the Highland Police Chief, so the line-up stays exactly as I told you in the first place. If anyone else tries to change anything, send them over to me." Again, we did as we were told. To be fair, I do not know if there was, or wasn't, a relevant reason for wanting to move the Chief Constable's car further up in the line, but I do know that a royal visit can make the most normal, intelligent people act in peculiar ways. Was I nervous that day? No, I really wasn't, but I was just a small cog in the wheel and had no direct contact with either the Queen or Prince Philip. And what if I were to be introduced to her? Well, however irrational, I have to admit that might have been a different story.

When you add this to conversations we have already had relating to the turmoil surrounding many of our past Scottish and English monarchs, I really can understand why so many of our guests are surprised that we never adopted the republican model. Of course, Britain did just that for a brief period in the mid-17th Century when, as you will recall, Charles I quite literally had his head removed, with Oliver Cromwell then becoming the "Lord Protector" and effectively a dictator. That term may not be entirely appropriate, as Cromwell had to be persuaded to take on the role, and realistically the absolutist monarch Charles I could equally have been described as a dictator. Had Cromwell's son Richard been a more willing and capable leader, history could well have taken a very different path and the Restoration may never have happened, though I am equally inclined to think that the people of England and Scotland are ultimately more comfortable with the idea of monarchy.

From this period onward, the real power of a monarch started to diminish in favour of Parliament, though any meaningful democracy was still a long way off. The divine right of kings, so cherished by the Stuart dynasty, was to disappear, and that was certainly the case by the time we reach the 18th Century Hanoverian line. Slowly but surely, monarchical power was eroded so that today the reigning monarch is a head of state who has to be seen to be above politics. Bearing in mind that most of my guests are from the USA, the question evolves to: "Okay, Jim, we get the history of royalty, but what is the point of them now?" The answer is really in the question, as it is the history of the evolution of British monarchy that maintains their relevance.

Although it could certainly be argued that the Glorious Revolution of 1688 was not particularly glorious, it did bring about a fundamental change in the way this country was, and is, governed. The subsequent 1689 Bill of Rights ensured that real power would thereafter lie with Parliament whilst the soft, symbolic power of the state would be retained by the monarchy, with the result that absolute power could no longer, and would never again, be invested in any one person, whether monarch or politician. Governments come and governments go according to the will of the people, but the monarchy remains a constant feature within the British State.

There is, of course, the occasional downside to having a

monarch as head of state. The most obvious being that, at the heart of this institution, there is a family like any other, and family relationships, as we all know, can be complicated. There have been – and doubtless will yet be – members within the royal family who have, deliberately or otherwise, created problematic issues of one kind or another, whether it was Caroline, the wife of George IV, Edward VII and Wallace Simpson, or more recently the tragic situation with Princess Diana. Now, in the early 21st Century, we have a royal second son whose dubious lifestyle, and even more dubious friendships, have understandably brought close scrutiny and, not for the first time, there are also younger family members who appear to be intent upon setting up an alternative "rival" royal court. Again, when you look at the history of royalty, none of this is new. It has all happened before. As I say, they are a family and, like all families, they find a way through.

Even the most fervent republican would have to concede that the reign of Elizabeth II (Elizabeth I of Scotland!) has been remarkably successful and her position is therefore pretty much unassailable. It will inevitably come to an end though, and the United Kingdom will enter the reign of Charles III, who has already indicated his intention to scale back the monarchy in terms of how many within the family will retain frontline royal duties. Whilst he will very likely receive public backing for such changes, it is already obvious that resistance to this will come from within the family. Modernising the institution of royalty is a slow but continuous process. Republicanism is still a minority viewpoint within the United Kingdom and has never really gained traction, even if it has risen slightly when the royal family have gone through periods of crisis, which all too often have been self-inflicted. However, there is a new aspect over which they have no control and that is the way in which living members of the royal family are now being portrayed in fictitious versions of their lives in major television productions. This has got to be worse than any level of negative press coverage, since damaging words are being spoken by actors; words that were almost certainly never uttered in real life, words that are insidiously dripping into the subconscious of the people watching. Historians of the future will see through this, but we all know how effective propaganda can be in the short term.

Some of my guests are not willing to buy into the historic foundation of our monarchical system and still feel that it is an unnecessary and costly institution. At first glance, it might be tempting to agree on the matter of cost, but again, it is worth taking a closer look. In 2017, a consultancy firm (Brand Finance Business Consultancy) concluded that the royal family contributed approximately £1.8 billion to the UK economy against a cost of £292 million. When it comes to marketing this country, they are a massive asset that cannot and should not be ignored. So, yes, having an unelected monarch as head of state in the 21st Century is a slightly ludicrous anomaly and, yes, the archaic pomp, ceremony, and deference can appear, and probably is at times, slightly ridiculous, but it is part of what makes the United Kingdom the country it is today and so far has served it extremely well.

29
Scottish Independence

In recent years, Scotland has gained prominence on the world stage due to a renewed emphasis on independence. As a result, many of my guests want to know more about Scotland's struggle to gain its freedom from the shackles of English rule, though admittedly, some who phrase the question in that way have perhaps overdosed on the film *Braveheart* and more recently the television series *Outlander*. You will hopefully not be surprised to hear that the reality is somewhat different, though not so different that some Scots still look upon William Wallace as an icon for Scottish independence and readily use his words (sorry, Mel Gibson's words): "They can take our lives, but they can never take our FREEDOM."

What about Jacobites? Do we still have Jacobites in Scotland? Given that it was a cause seeking to re-establish a specific monarchical line, I am not sure there is a contemporary equivalent of Jacobitism though some people may try to establish a link by connecting it to one of the various strands of the original Jacobite cause; the most obvious being the desire to end the union that created the United Kingdom. On that basis, we could perhaps glibly suggest that a few, albeit very few, among those who now support Scottish independence might be classed as modern-day Jacobites though admittedly that would be to follow the same kind of logic as my American friend who posed the question, "Was William Wallace a Jacobite?" by implying a level of genericism that does not really exist. Virtually every guest I have toured with during the last six/seven years has been keen to understand contemporary Scotland's apparent preoccupation with independence and that cannot really be achieved without at least some discussion relating to the background of the issues involved. More often than not, it sparks off one of our great conversations though I also have to admit it is one of those subjects that does not necessarily hold universal interest. The few guests who fall into the latter category tend to give out visible clues such as when their eyes start to glaze over, and they gradually take on an appearance that clearly indicates they are slowly but surely losing the will to live. Politics can do that to some people.

As we know, the 1707 Act of Union that brought Scotland, England, and Wales into a United Kingdom was extremely unpopular in its early years, though it eventually settled down and the desire for a return to Scottish independence almost disappeared – almost, but never completely. When it did arise, discussion would centre around the idea of home rule rather than complete separation, as was the case with Ireland, where, by the latter part of the 19th Century, the idea was gathering ever-greater momentum. As the system of true democratic government started to mature, the Tories took on the name of the Conservative Party, and the Whigs became the Liberal Party, though splits and breakaway groups did occur. However, both parties were still made up of the wealthy "ruling class" and that did not change till the arrival of the Labour Party in the very early 20th Century. Coinciding as it did with an extension of the voting franchise, it marked the beginning of a permanent shift in United Kingdom politics. The working-class vote gradually swung behind Labour and, as a result, the Liberals ceased to be a major force. The Scottish National Party fully came into existence in 1934 under the leadership of a gentleman by the name of John MacCormick, who actually sought more government autonomy for Scotland rather than outright independence. Under later leadership, that policy would change, and thereafter the goal would become, and remain, one of outright independence. Around this time, Conservatives went under the heading of the Conservative and Unionist Party though in Scotland they dropped the word "Conservative" and simply went under the heading of the Unionist Party, which was presumably in recognition of the difference between Scottish and English politics.

The Unionist (Conservative) Party were the leading force in Scottish politics during the first half of the 20th Century, with the Labour Party providing the main opposition and the separate Liberal Party now pretty much in the "also ran" category. At that time, the Scottish nationalists were little more than a protest group. All this was to change in the second half of the century, as by the 1960s, it was the Labour Party that was in the dominant position; they not only sent the largest block of MPs to the Westminster Parliament but also started to take control of local government in the poorer urban areas of Scotland. The Scottish National Party (SNP) were still a minor political force, but they did occasionally break to the surface, so the issue of Scottish independence could not be totally ignored. However, they made a real breakthrough in the 1974 general election when they had eleven MPs elected to the Westminster Parliament and this almost certainly came about due to the discovery of oil in the North Sea. Though it was not enough to cause any great panic in political circles, it did bring about a new focus on Scotland and undoubtedly concentrated minds.

A referendum on Scottish devolution, that was initially proposed by a Conservative Government but enacted by a Labour Government, finally took place in 1979 though it was subject to achieving a threshold of 40% of all registered voters. The actual result was 51.6% for devolution and 48.4% against, but the Yes vote represented only 32.8% of the entire voting population, so it could not be passed. By virtue of the 40% threshold, those who did not vote counted as a No. It was a later Labour Party leader, the respected Scotsman John Smith, who came to describe this as "unfinished business".

The Labour Party Government in Westminster were reliant upon the support of the eleven SNP members to remain in power, but following the debacle of the devolution referendum, the SNP withdrew their support and forced a general election, which was won by the Conservative Party and, in the process, made history when their leader, Margaret Thatcher, became the first ever female prime minister of the United Kingdom. It would probably be fair to say that the United Kingdom in general had a kind of love/hate relationship with Mrs Thatcher, but it might equally be fair to say that Scotland ended up having a hate/hate relationship with her. In many policy areas, she was to the right of centre and that did not go down well in a Scotland that was largely left of centre, at least in comparison with most of the population in England. Rightly or wrongly, she will forever be linked to the de-industrialisation of Scotland that gathered pace during her premiership, but even more so, the Thatcher name is synonymous with a replacement local government tax regime introduced by her administration – the dreaded poll tax. Basically, it was a flat-rate, regressive tax that appeared to favour the wealthiest in society, so anathema to most Scots. To supporters of Scottish nationalism, this was clear evidence of a democratic deficit, as yet again, the people of Scotland were having policies thrust upon them by a government, and a prime minister, they would never have voted for. Scotland, at that time, voted overwhelmingly for the more left-leaning Labour Party, who by now saw themselves as the "Party of Scotland" and almost certainly believed their position was unassailable. Mrs Thatcher's government chose to first introduce the poll tax in Scotland before rolling it out in the rest of the United Kingdom the following year. Even though that decision was mostly down to Scottish office ministers within the Conservative Government, it would be Mrs Thatcher, as prime minister, who would ultimately shoulder the blame for apparently using Scotland as a "test bed" for this extremely unpopular new tax.

The howls of protest in Scotland against the poll tax were completely ignored, so as planned, the policy was introduced in England the following year, where resistance was louder, larger, and at times, violent. It was a massive political miscalculation and the UK Government very quickly had to do an about turn and go back to the property-based system for raising local taxes. It was also a disaster for the Conservative Party that ultimately destroyed Mrs Thatcher's premiership. You can imagine what this did for the SNP, who were all too aware that they no longer needed to prove there was a democratic deficit, as they now claimed that the Conservative Government and prime minister had provided all the evidence that could ever be required. Whilst it is worth emphasising that the hated poll tax was very far from being the single issue that drove Scotland towards nationalism, it was, without question, a significant event on that journey.

On a United Kingdom basis, the Labour Party had spent most of the 1980s in the wilderness, as they had moved so far to the left they were basically unelectable. It took a series of new leaders to try and turn that particular ship around though the process got a massive shot in the arm when Tony Blair took over as leader in 1994 following the sudden death of John Smith. He and his supporters brought their party to a centre-left position and sold themselves as "New Labour". Three years later, he became prime minister when, in the 1997 general election, the Labour Party won with a massive landslide. Conversely, it was, of course, a disaster for the Conservative Party, especially in Scotland, where their vote plummeted to the extent that they did not achieve a single parliamentary seat. Whatever government was in power at Westminster, the Labour Party had retained its position as the dominant force in Scottish politics, but they were under constant threat from the SNP. Tony Blair's new government clearly wanted to hold on to their Scottish power base, so chose to immediately honour a pledge they had made to hold another referendum in Scotland on the subject of devolution. This was the late John Smith's "unfinished business"

In September 1997, the people of Scotland again went to polling stations, this time to vote Yes or No to the creation of a devolved "Scottish Assembly". Every political party, with the exception of the Conservatives, actively campaigned for a Yes vote. The turnout was high, and the Yes vote achieved a remarkable 74.2%, so the following year, this new political body came into existence. It was not independence, but it returned a great deal of decision making back to Scotland that would be overseen by an executive body made up of 129 members, voted for by the Scottish public. Matters relating to foreign policy, general taxation policy, and other "important" issues would remain with the Westminster Parliament, where Scotland would still enjoy the same representation it had always done, which in itself, was a bit of a problem. Many now questioned the right of Scottish members in the Westminster Parliament to vote on matters in England such as health and education where they no longer represented their own constituents, as responsibility for this now lay with the Scottish Executive. This was highlighted when Dr John Reid, a Westminster MP elected in a Scottish Constituency, was given the position of Health Minister in Tony Blair's government. As the senior minister in that department, he was responsible for all major decisions relating to the health service in England, but he had zero influence in Scotland, where he was elected, as all matters relating to health had been devolved to the new Scottish Executive and the elected MSPs (Member of the Scottish Parliament). Is it any surprise that the phrase "English votes for English laws" now entered the political vocabulary? Even today, it is an issue without a resolution.

Round about this stage in our conversation, many of my American guests come up with a question along the following lines: "Okay, Jim, is it fair to say that the United Kingdom has always favoured what we would call big government?" To which I have to answer: "Yes." They then add: "So you are now telling us that Scotland deliberately chose to add yet another layer of government?" To which I have to answer: "Err, yes." Sometimes the short answer is the only one you can give.

While there were many in the Labour Party who genuinely believed in the policy of devolving more power to a democratically elected Scottish Executive, there were undoubtedly many others who saw it more in terms of halting the rise of the SNP. However, there were a number of politicians from across the political spectrum who believed that, far from destroying the SNP, the advent of a separate Scottish Parliament would actually create a platform upon which the SNP would build. They were right.

The first elections for the Scottish Parliament took place in May 1999 when its 129 members were elected under a proportional representation system which was clearly designed to ensure that no single party could gain a dominant majority. The Labour Party still held sway in Scotland, which meant it was no surprise when they gained the most seats, though not enough to form an administration, so they had to go into a coalition with the much smaller Liberal Party. Perhaps the biggest surprise, for some at least, was the substantial support for the SNP who, as the second largest group, became the official opposition.

The voting system of proportional representation also served to revive the fortunes of the Conservative Party in Scotland and allowed them to, again, find a voice. Under the very able leadership of Alex Salmond, the SNP had, for some time, been moving to a left of centre position and, as a result, began to make huge inroads into the Labour vote, which was now on a rapidly downward spiral. In subsequent elections, the SNP capitalised on this and, against all the odds, won control of the Scottish Parliament, with Mr Salmond taking over as Scotland's First Minister. Although early administrations were known as the Scottish Executive, the SNP now rebranded it officially as the Scottish Parliament, which to be fair, most people had been calling it anyway.

Bearing in mind that the raison d'être of the SNP is full independence for Scotland, it was no surprise that, having gained an outright majority in the 2011 election, they would then push for a referendum on that very subject, and equally no surprise that it was something the United Kingdom Government could no longer refuse. The independence referendum was held in September of 2014 and proved to be extremely divisive, to the extent that some families were split between for and against. It also sharpened any divide between Scotland and England, as the thought of Scottish independence gave rise to a new form of English nationalism.

During that summer, I had been touring with a couple in both Scotland and England when, on our way south, we stopped at York, where a walking tour had been organised with a York city guide. Needless to say, we had many great conversations during our trip that, of course, included the subject of the forthcoming independence vote, and I was fairly certain it would also crop up during their walking tour, as it really was at the forefront of everyone's mind at that time. When the York guide returned with the couple, he turned to me and said: "Don't worry, I have told these people the truth about this referendum, that if the Scots go ahead and vote for independence, they will soon come running back when they no longer have England to subsidise them." Despite the fact that I was not then, and am still not, convinced of the merits of independence, I have to admit that I was angered by this comment, to the extent that I would have fired back with both barrels had the guests not been present. There has never been any doubt in my mind that Scotland was, and is, perfectly capable of self-government, so the question for me, and many others, is more about whether or not it would be the right thing to do. It should be recognised that there is a difference between patriotism and nationalism though the line between these two positions became somewhat blurred during the 2014 referendum on Scottish independence and sadly has remained so ever since. As the referendum day drew closer, there was a general recognition that the vote was going to be close, and it was. By a margin of 55% to 45%, Scotland chose not to vote for independence. Surely this would, for some time, mean the end of the independence debate? No, as it turns out, it most definitely would not.

Maybe the people of Scotland did not want full independence, but they were still determined to elect SNP politicians to both the Scottish and United Kingdom parliaments. Scotland continued to turn away from the once dominant Labour Party, as it was now the SNP who utterly dominated Scottish politics.

In June of 2016, the United Kingdom voted, by a narrow majority, to leave the European Union. Well, actually, it was not really the whole of the United Kingdom, as Scotland, if accounted for separately, voted by a significant majority to remain within the European Union, so the stage was set for the resurrection of the Scottish independence debate on the basis that Scotland was being dragged out of the EU against the wishes of its people. Will there be another referendum on Scottish independence? The likely answer is yes and, had it not been for Covid, it may well have taken place in 2021. What will the result be next time? I, for one, have absolutely no idea, but we can, unfortunately, be pretty certain that bitterly divisive politics will remain as a feature of life in Scotland for some time to come though sadly, in that respect, Scotland is far from unique.

Like many others, I am frequently tempted to indulge in "armchair politics", but in truth, my personal experience of real politicians, from all parties, has left me with great admiration for the job they do. From around 1995 to 2015, we regularly provided car services to various government agencies and that often meant driving senior government ministers, who we found, with few exceptions, to be incredibly hardworking, highly motivated, well-intentioned people with a genuine belief in what they were doing. Brian Wilson, a well-known figure in the Highlands, certainly falls into that category. He was another MP, elected in Scotland, who went on to hold high office in Tony Blair's government, but despite being a prominent member of the Labour Party, he never made any secret of his opposition to the whole idea of a devolved Scottish Parliament. In later years, he concluded that, by delivering a Scottish Parliament, the Labour

Party had, in effect, constructed its own scaffold. He could have added that they set Scotland on a journey to a destination that is, as yet, still unknown.

During most touring journeys, I frequently talk to my guests about King Edward I, Hammer of the Scots, who in the early 14th Century tried and, due to resistance from great warriors such as William Wallace and Robert the Bruce, failed to unite the kingdoms of Scotland and England. During the many miles we travel through this beautiful little country, our conversations cover the turbulent centuries that followed, including the early 17th Century when, by entirely peaceful means, the Crowns of England and Scotland were united, and the early 18th Century when, by political negotiation, Scotland and England finally came together to form the United Kingdom. As we know, the violent struggle of the Jacobite cause failed to reverse that union, but now in the 21st Century, our conversations again turn to the possible destruction of the United Kingdom. At the risk of invoking the "Auld Alliance", I am inclined towards a statement from the 19th Century French writer and critic Jean-Baptiste Alphonse Karr: "The more things change, the more they are the same."